The
Psychology Of
Spiritual
Growth

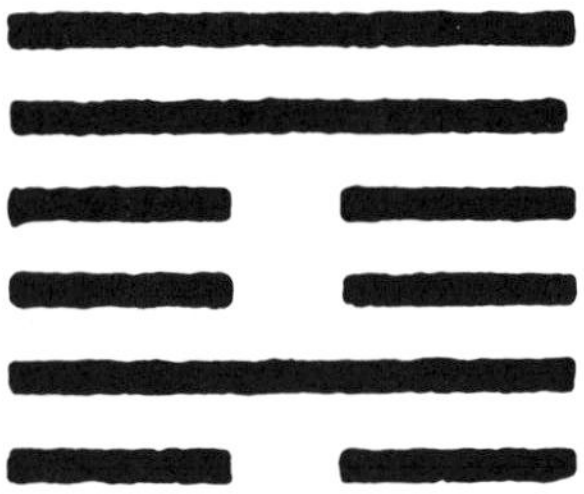

The Psychology Of Spiritual Growth

Channelled from the Brotherhood
by Mary E. Carreiro

A Gentle Wind Book

Bergin & Garvey Publishers, Inc.
Massachusetts

First published in 1987 by
Bergin & Garvey Publishers, Inc.
670 Amherst Road
South Hadley, Massachusetts 01075

789   987654321

Printed in the Unites States of America
Library of Congress Cataloging-in-Publiction Data

Carreiro, Mary Elizabeth.
   The psychology of spiritual growth.

   1. Gentle Wind Retreat (Organization : Kittery, Me.)
2. Brotherhood (Brothers and Sisters of the Inner World)
3. Spiritual healing.   4. Spiritual life.   I. Title.
BP605.G44C37   1987   131   86-20799
ISBN 0-89789-123-6
ISBN 0-89789-124-4 (pbk.)

Contents

Preface

THIS BOOK REPRESENTS the first in a series of books being offered to humanity by the Brotherhood. The Brotherhood is a group of souls, both men and women, who live primarily in the nonphysical world. These souls are dedicated to helping humanity out of their current pain and suffering through a process of spiritual growth called evolution.

The Brothers and Sisters of the Inner World are here to teach humanity about the need for evolution and about the nature of each soul. They are here to offer a healing technology to restore the human consciousness to a state of balance and peace. This information and the healing technology are being offered through a physical world community called Gentle Wind Retreat. Gentle Wind is located in southern Maine. It is not a "retreat" center in the usual sense. It is more like a school and research center for this evolutionary project. All of the staff members maintain continuous telepathic communication with the Brotherhood. The community members receive these communications and then use this information to construct and manufacture a series of healing instruments which are discussed in several chapters. They also receive information such as the data contained in this book, as well as individual soul readings which are also discussed in this book.

A healing instrument and a soul reading can be obtained by writing to Gentle Wind for information. No one can ever be charged a fee for these instruments or the soul readings. This community is mandated by spiritual law to serve all in humanity. People are asked to make whatever donations they can in order to support the project and insure that this work continues.

To obtain more information about Gentle Wind and the services offered, write or call:

> Gentle Wind Retreat
> P.O. Box 387
> Kittery, ME 03904
>
> 1-(207) 439-5620

Call between 9 a.m. and 7 p.m., seven days a week.

Introduction

THE LONG AGE of Darkness, a period of almost 75,000 years, has come to a close. A new era of spiritual regeneration and growth has begun. The years of endarkenment, however, have left humanity without purpose and without the means to accomplish genuine spiritual growth.

The Brotherhood, a group of male and female souls dedicated to the evolution of humanity, is here to offer the necessary information and healing technology so that spiritual growth can once again be achieved. The information contained in this book is channelled directly from the Brotherhood under the guidance of the Planetary Logos. It is offered at this time as a practical guide for those who wish to undertake the hard work and personal sacrifices required for evolutionary gain. Evolution is a specific process of learning and growing through continuous change, directed and engineered by the individual soul. It is a process of accumulating information and skills that allow the soul to lift itself up to higher and more peaceful states of existence.

Evolution has nothing to do with personal growth experiences, mind expansion, personality development or human success. This is not a book for psychotherapists, New Age philosophers, or technique seekers of any kind. The Brotherhood is concerned only with the growth of the soul, not the human ego.

This book has nothing to do with religion since religion has nothing to do with spiritual growth. The Brotherhood does not offer a set of rituals to practice or dogmas to believe. Religious rituals and dogmas have only caused souls to lose sight of individual purpose and to venture further into aimlessness and spiritual despair.

This book is a simple guide to the real process of evolution. It is here to aid souls back to a path of continuous, purposeful spiritual growth. Over 98 percent of the souls on this planet are now wandering from lifetime to lifetime, perpetuating their damages, pain and suffering without any growth whatsoever. Social, economic and political systems everywhere continue to support this human suffering without any concern for evolution. People are bombarded every day with media campaigns to remain endarkened. They are encouraged to become more glamourous, more successful, more powerful, without any regard for the condition of anyone's soul.

The Brotherhood works only on behalf of souls and promises to remain on this planet until each and every soul has been restored to a path of spiritual growth. This book is part of a specific project, directed by the Planetary Logos, aimed at fulfilling that promise to provide support and aid.

Ultimately, however, the pace of evolution is determined by individual free will. Most of humanity misuses free will to sustain the comforts of the human ego and to avoid confrontation with anything that would promote soul advancement. Many who read this information will be angered. Some will be shocked and perhaps insulted. Others will be inspired, and still others will prefer to live with their limited vision and small ideas.

Regardless of one's human reaction or spiritual commitment, there is still only one purpose for incarnating and that purpose is evolution. Those who read this book are free to be angry, shocked, confused, insulted, disgusted, inspired, or anything else they would like to be. The Brotherhood will simply wait for each soul no matter how long it takes. This may take a year, a lifetime or fifty lifetimes, but sooner or later all souls are destined to return home.

1

THE HUMAN CONDITION

HUMANITY EXISTS ONLY so that evolution can be accomplished. The planet earth exists solely to provide a physical world where evolution can occur. The inhabitants of this planet come here for the single purpose of accomplishing evolution, a process of ongoing spiritual growth.

Humanity suffers from ignorance and purposelessness—products of 75,000 years of endarkenment. The Age of Darkness has left humanity unconscious, misinformed and aimless. People simply do not know why they are on this planet. Each day people go about their lives without any understanding of what they are doing on earth in physical bodies. They do not know how they got here, why they are here, or what happens to them when their bodies die. It is as though people everywhere are drugged and asleep and cannot wake themselves up to reality. They are like robots. They believe in religious fantasies of heaven and hell, and of stagnant lives dedicated to meaningless notions of human success.

Most people believe that they are their bodies and their minds. They do not even know they *have* souls, nevermind the actual fact that they *are* souls. This unconsciousness and ignorance causes people to spend thousands of years incarnating without any spiritual growth at all. How can people possibly grow spiritually when they do not even know why they are here? Before people can grow they must penetrate the mystery of life itself, the purpose for living in the first place.

Darkness has truly left people drugged, in a drunken stupor, unable to awaken until now. People say they can no longer settle for aimlessness, for religious fantasies and for painful or mediocre lives. Yet, the awakening for many will be a great shock. People will not want to see why they are here. They will not want to hear that evolution is the only game in town. They will want to keep things the same, even though their lives may be very difficult. People will not want to discover that they are automatically playing in the game of evolution just by being here in incarnation. However, only by accepting the fact that evolution is the only real reason for being here, can one successfully accomplish spiritual growth and know anything about playing in the game.

Evolution is a process of growth through change that is directed and engineered by the individual soul. Each soul has its own destination, its own cause for existence. Evolution is governed by spiritual law and guided by Planetary Hierarchy. The Brotherhood exists to aid and support souls seeking spiritual growth.

Because people do not know the game they are playing, they do not know how to play by the rules of spiritual law. They cannot hear their souls. They live by their parents' rules of life or by church laws, both of which lead souls away from spiritual growth by continuing the automatic responses of the human personality.

The soul is the life force. It is the only part of the person that survives at each physical death. It is the only "permanent" part of the person, designed to accomplish specific requirements for ongoing growth. Some requirements may be fulfilled in a single lifetime, while others may take hundreds of years. However, if done correctly, each successive lifetime offers the necessary situations for those requirements to be fulfilled.

People do not yet believe, however, that they *are* their souls. They spend their lives tending to their bodies, emotions, thoughts and desires. They seek something "permanent," but they are always looking in the temporary material world.

People try to establish stability through marriage, home, children, or career. They seek physical comfort and sameness. They do not seek spiritual growth which requires change and discomfort. Most human beings live like robots that automatically do the same thing everyday. They believe they are successful if they can stay with the same company for forty years or with the same marriage partner for fifty years. They seek stagnation rather than movement, and believe they are doing the right thing.

There are people who believe they are changing, especially people who go to New Age workshops and attend psychotherapy sessions. In most cases, these "changes" are not changes that produce spiritual growth. They are simply alterations in the human personality. These alterations are designed by the human ego to help "cope" with damages and avoid confrontation with genuine spiritual growth. Because these alterations are not directed or engineered by the soul, they generally lead only to new approaches to the same chronic problems and behavior patterns.

Evolution is not a process of coping with pain but rather it is a process of being lifted, by the soul, out of human pain and suffering. Spiritual growth does not require mental analysis of one's relationships or life problems. The human mind is far too inadequate to accomplish the demands and requirements for soul evolution. The human mind only contains a computerized system of present life events that are, for most people, unrelated to the destiny of the soul. The soul has lifetimes worth of information that can guide and direct the physical vehicle to solve present life problems and to learn from these events. For most people, however, the human mind and the human personality are much louder than the soul. Therefore, people live without the benefits of soul memory and soul guidance, directed instead by the dictates of the human ego.

THE HUMAN PERSONALITY

The human personality is a composite of all the preferences, ideas, damages, desires, feelings and thoughts that comprise an individual consciousness. The personality is a function of the natal astrological influences combined with past and present life experiences. People have become very interested in developing and improving their personalities. They attend various weekend workshops, psychotherapies and classes so that they can become even more proficient at being a human personality. Some people want to become better managers and executives. Others want to gain more control. Some strive to become more romantic and desirable sexual partners. Many seek new "communication" skills, and others want new approaches to old relationships. People are willing to pay a lot of money to "improve" themselves. They are willing to exercise beyond their physical capacities and to diet until they are malnourished. But very few on this planet have any interest in improving their souls. In fact, most people take better care of almost everything in their lives, leaving their souls with little or no support.

The human personality has gained a stronghold on most people because the Age of Darkness has left so many wounded and hurt. When a person is damaged by some painful life event or events, those damages remain in that person's consciousness until they are healed. Further, the damages act like magnetic energies that continue to attract more of the same. For example, people tend to repeat the same painful relationship patterns no matter how hard they try not to do so.

The human personality is "developed" to protect damages and wounds and to keep oneself from incurring more hurt and pain. Ironically, this system never works and personalities are actually used by the human ego to continue the pain and damage.

For example, Michael's chief complaint (everybody has one or two) is that he cannot keep a relationship for more than six months and that the women in his life are always leaving him. Somewhere along the line he decides that if he could improve himself—his ability to relate, his "love making" skills—then he would have more productive, healthier relationships. He spends years in psychotherapy and thousands of dollars at New Age workshops designed to help him with his problem. Years later Michael is still unable to maintain a relationship. He has "developed" and "improved" his personality and perhaps he has grown, but not at the level of the soul. The human ego has grown—larger and more cumbersome.

If humanity could see through the eyes of the Inner World they would see that Michael is wounded, hurt and in a constant state of imbalance. They would see that Michael carries these wounds energetically in his consciousness. They would see dark spots in his aura and breaks in the meridian system where the damage is held.

If humanity could see into Michael's records of the past, they would find that he had lost a wife and two children in a terrible fire that occurred many thousands of years ago. These tragedies left him broken-hearted and the results of these losses were never properly healed. Michael lives in fear everyday that he will lose his loved ones. He clings to them, suffocating and choking them emotionally. He holds so tightly to the women in his life that they all leave him, complaining about his possessiveness and emotional suppression. Michael's whole life is directed out of these damages. The human personality attempts to protect him from further hurt. Yet, he suffers from one lost love after another, all chased away by his own fear and hurt.

Michael's pain acts like a magnetic attraction force. He pulls to himself women with similar damages or corresponding pain. He finds women who do not like him, or other men for that matter. He attracts women who suffer from their own fears of loss that lead them into the same kinds of suffocating relationships.

When his relationships end he feels the hurt and loss, but decides that he is simply being victimized by women who do not appreciate him. He has thoughts about finding the "right" woman and actually believes he has just not been searching long enough. He cannot face his own pain long enough to see that he has driven women out of his life. In his words, "I just haven't found someone who really wants to commit at a deep enough level to make a relationship work."

His psychotherapy sessions and weekend workshops have not helped him because none of these offer humanity the necessary technology to properly heal such damage. Michael has simply adjusted further into his damage, covering his fears and hurts with sophisticated words about relationships and more mental junk to wade through. Michael cannot see that his life is one long, chronic, repetitive behavior pattern. He is not learning anything. Everything is exactly the same. And worse than this, he has probably been doing exactly the same thing for hundreds of years without any spiritual growth at all.

Spiritual growth can only be accomplished when the voice of the soul can be heard. The soul can guide and direct the vehicle toward change and growth. In order to evolve, the soul must have some level of control over the human personality. In most cases, however, the human personality has the control and directs the physical vehicle so that people cannot change and grow in productive ways. Most people are too busy protecting their damages and projecting their problems onto others to actually see the sources of their own difficulty. Some people are simply too damaged to be able to look at themselves. It is just not "humanly" possible.

In order, then, for evolution to occur, people must be healed of past pain and suffering. They must be healed in a way that energetically reaches the sources of the pain, and that by-passes the mental chatter of the human personality. We, the Brotherhood, offer humanity such a technology to accomplish this healing process. Unlike psychotherapy and New Age "improvement" workshops that fruitlessly attempt to heal people by talking about or "experiencing" their problems, the technology from the Brotherhood works directly with the soul. People have already "experienced" enough pain. The work of the Brotherhood is to heal humanity and to alleviate the damage and suffering so that souls can once again be heard.

TECHNOLOGY

Gentle Wind Retreat, a small community of people living in Maine, acts as the distribution center for healing instruments designed by the Brotherhood and guided by the Planetary Logos. The actual project has existed in the Inner World (the nonphysical world) for many thousands of years. Many souls have contributed to the research and design of the healing tools now manufactured by Gentle Wind.

The tools are constructed out of present day acrylics, metals, wood and various other materials that are inexpensive and easily accessible. The information about the materials to be used, the design, and the formulas are all communicated telepathically from the Inner World to members of the Gentle Wind Community. Blueprints are drawn up and instruments are then constructed according to exact specifications from the Inner World.

The instruments are usually small enough to be held in one hand and are available to anyone seeking the aid of the Brotherhood (see Preface for mailing information). They are designed to energetically heal the damages in the consciousness. They cause the personality to reconnect with the soul and set in motion the changes required for spiritual growth. Here, we will focus on the disintegration of past and present life damages.

The damages themselves exist in the aura, the energy outside and surrounding the physical body. The damages are not in the mind, as psychotherapists might believe. So the Brotherhood does not treat the mind. The damages are not sourced in the physical body, although they might affect the body. The damages are held energetically in the web that surrounds the body and pass with the soul from one lifetime to the next until they are properly treated.

The instruments are constructed according to the specifications of the Brotherhood. They each contain certain herbs and cell salts that energetically react in the human consciousness when combined with specific shapes and lines. The human mind cannot comprehend "how" these instruments work because the Brotherhood is working with humanity in subatomic areas unknown to people at this time.

The healing instruments have their own history and evolution, neither of which is the focus of this work. It is only necessary that people know these instruments exist; that the instruments come from the Brotherhood guided by the Logos; and that they allow people to be healed so that evolution can once again occur. It must be understood that healing one's damages does not necessarily cause evolution. Healing the damages only allows for the possibility of evolution. Healing the damages gives a person the opportunity to quiet the human personality and to stop the chronic, repetitive patterns that prevent spiritual growth. Evolution only occurs through the accomplishment of certain spiritual requirements necessary for continued growth. Because humanity has lived in darkness for so long, the hurts and the suffering are too loud for humanity to quiet. Souls cannot be heard through the noise and pain. Only when the voice of the soul is heard can a person respond to the directives of that soul and thus grow spiritually.

It must be understood that even removing the damages and quieting the consciousness will not necessarily produce evolution. Removing the sources of a person's chronic pain and suffering is only a prerequisite for evolution. Quieting the consciousness only allows for the possibility of evolution. People must want to grow spiritually and must be willing to sacrifice their own ideas about success and personal happiness.

This technology will alleviate the chronic pain and suffering in people, and it will dissolve the damaged areas of the consciousness, eliminating the magnetic attraction to others with like damage. However, this technology cannot interfere with free will nor can it eliminate ideas. In fact, the healing instruments actually allow people to be more of what is normal and natural to them, personality traits determined by their natal astrological chart.

Let us consider again the example of Michael. Michael has suffered a great deal in his life because his past hurts and losses were so much in control. He was unable to attract healthy women who liked him, and unable to stop himself from all the negative, suppressive behavior patterns. A great deal of energy was spent trying to protect himself from the source of his suffering.

The technology of the Brotherhood will give Michael the opportunity to regain control of his life. He will no longer suffer from the chronic hurt of the past. However, this does not mean that Michael will want to grow spiritually. That is always unknown. Whether he will sacrifice his incorrect ideas and elaborate behavior patterns becomes a matter of free will—a matter that remains sacred to each in humanity.

FREE WILL

Free will is often thought of as an individual's ability to choose. In a limited sense this is correct. Humanity does not yet understand the nature of will and therefore does not comprehend its energetic nature. It is true that each person maintains free will and that always humanity is free to choose each individual course of evolution. It is true that the Brotherhood does not interfere with any of humanity's choices. However, will is not a concept of the mind nor is it an idea of freedom. Will is an energetic act. In a simple sense, each person must will themselves out of bed in the morning. For some, this act requires only a minimal use of will. For others, this act requires a great deal of will. In either case a certain amount of energy must be expended.

Free will, then, is energy expended. Some people will use their energy to become famous or wealthy or successful in the human sense. These are not bad goals. They simply have nothing to do with spiritual growth. They have only to do with human growth. Free will used in these circumstances might be thought of as human will. Most people on this planet have developed a strong human will. They have done so to protect themselves from both past life damages and present day hurts. In fact, most so-called "free will" is automatically used to protect damage and to promote some compensation for the damage. An example might be a woman whom we shall call Jane, who has past lives of physical abuse and powerlessness. She now uses all her will and talent to insure a present life executive position in a company that allows her to abuse people through her management style. Jane misuses her will and therefore does not promote her own evolution. She is "strong-willed" but only in the human sense. From the Brotherhood's point of view she is spiritually negligent.

A few people on this planet actually seek evolution above human success. They know they are here only to be directed by their souls. By answering the directions of the soul, spiritual growth is possible. This form of free will is spiritual will. Spiritual will means that a person uses his or her energy on behalf of the soul rather than on behalf of the human personality.

Many New Age technologies offer incorrect information about free will, because a vast portion of these so-called technologies know nothing of spiritual growth. They only know of human ego growth. These technologies teach people such misconceptions as "anything is possible, if you try." This is not a spiritual notion. It is a human notion and one that is even incorrect as a human idea. "Anything" is not possible for everyone. Talent is necessary, and in most cases where failures occur talent is lacking in the human sense. This incorrect idea leads people to take up running marathons or walking on hot coals, actually believing that these things are related to their souls. They are not. Running marathons is a complete misuse of will in 99 percent of the cases. People dedicated to genuine spiritual growth do not attempt to grow spiritually by overexerting their bodies. This is absurd.

Perhaps a more absurd notion is the idea that one accomplishes growth by walking on hot coals. This experience is not only completely unnatural and a gross misuse of will, but it also fractures the consciousness in such a serious way that most "coalwalkers" will take lifetimes to heal before any evolution can resume. Humanity develops new opportunities for misusing free will every year. There are more ways to misuse will now and there will be even more in the future.

Then there are those who do not connect with their own will. They believe they are not connected to the outcomes of their lives. They think of themselves as passengers who sit in the back seat of life being driven by life from one place to another. They refuse to see that they are in the driver's seat. They refuse to accept responsibility for their driving. When their lives crash into others or break down because of their poor driving, they blame life and do not see that each and every act is an act of will.

Will sets the ideas of humanity into motion. Human beings have many ideas about what will bring personal happiness. Most of these are incorrect and lead to one dissatisfaction after another. Ideas start out as thoughtforms. Then people pump energy into these thoughtforms until they become full-blown ideas. Then, the ideas are set into motion. The energy that is pumped into an idea comes from will. It is an act of will. The energy that sets an idea into motion is also an act of will.

When some ideas are set into motion they are like rocks being rolled down a hill. The idea sits on top of the hill until it amasses enough energy to roll off the top and head for the bottom. People do not see that they are pushing the rocks off the hill through the use of their wills. People act like they have nothing to do with their ideas. This phenomenon is very understandable since most human ideas roll wildly down the hill and crash into dissatisfaction at the bottom. However, because people do not want to be responsible for their ideas—to see that they alone have set their ideas into motion—they chronically repeat the same unsuccessful ideas, getting the same unsuccessful results. They are continually going "back to the drawing board" to create another unsuccessful idea for personal happiness. These ideas are dictated by the demands of the human personality with no regard for spiritual success and happiness whatsoever.

This continuous pattern is normal for humanity and represents the vast misuse of free will. Each human ego demand is propelled by human will. Each time a human idea is fulfilled, the soul is robbed of the energy that was used to fulfill this idea. Each time the human ego wins, the soul loses, because human will has overpowered spiritual will.

It must also be understood that there are people who simply do not want to grow in any way. They usually live comfortable lives and strongly prefer to keep their lives exactly that way. They do not wish to have their pleasures disturbed. They do not want to be inconvenienced by personal sacrifices. Their lives are not necessarily great, they are just stable and comfortable, without change and without growth.

These people often have not suffered severe damages and do not live in pain. They have used their free will to establish a steady income, good home, stable job. They have found the right neighborhoods with comfortable neighbors close to "good" schools. They do not wish to see anything else but these tiny, little worlds of human comfort. They are not in pain so they do not seek relief. They are without motivation to change and have no desire to keep moving in the way that spiritual evolution requires. They know nothing of their own souls and prefer not to know.

Comfortable people often misuse free will for hundreds and even thousands of years. They use it to prevent or ward off any situation that would challenge their personal comfort and potentially cause spiritual growth. They will not sacrifice anything. Some believe that by contributing money or donating some spare time to a volunteer endeavor they are fulfilling their obligations to society. They are not. Their contributions and volunteerism only buy them the right to remain comfortable. Their contributions are made out of personal convenience, not out of a desire to serve humanity. In one sense, they are often the best equipped to serve because they are relatively healthy. But they do not wish to serve or to feel the suffering in anyone else's life unless it is personally convenient. So, although as a group they are the least damaged, they are also the least likely to aid humanity in the spiritual restoration process. They have willed themselves into complete comfort and stagnation. They place far greater value on their golf games and tax deductions than they do on their spiritual growth.

EVOLUTION

Evolution is a process of ongoing spiritual growth and learning. Each soul on this planet is here for a specific purpose. Each soul has an original cause for existence. And, each soul is here to fulfill that purpose and to ultimately return to its spiritual home.

Humanity thinks of souls in religious terms and relates to the soul from false notions of heaven or hell. There are no such places as humanity conceives them. The only "hell" humanity is destined to know is right here on earth and on the lower astral planes. This is as dark and as hurtful as things can get because souls are so lost, damaged, and off purpose.

Each soul originates from a spiritual home that could be thought of as its Celestial Origin. Human souls connected to the planet earth originate from one of six possible spheres of Celestial Origin. There are billions of other souls from other planets and other galaxies that originate from other places. Human minds are too limited and mis-informed to comprehend the indefinite number of souls and vast planes of existence.

Each human soul carries an energetic impression, a symbol, that represents that soul's purpose for being here. Each soul carries its own unique symbol and each soul has its own individual purpose. All souls exist as part of a much larger plan.

In order for souls to fulfill their destinies, certain spiritual re-quirements must be met. These requirements usually take many, many lifetimes to fulfill. Because the Age of Darkness has left hu-manity so completely disconnected from their souls, very few souls are fulfilling any requirements for spiritual growth. Souls are gen-erally wandering from one lifetime to another without any control over the physical vehicle they are connected with, unable to learn anything of spiritual value.

Under ideal circumstances, each soul would guide the physical vehicle into situations that would promote spiritual growth. The human ego would be understood for its nature and would cooperate to a much greater extent with the will of the soul. People would know they are here in the physical world because it can provide so many opportunities for evolution. They would know that this is the only purpose of the physical plane and would therefore have little or no interest in gaining power, money, glamour or any of the existing entrapments.

Under ideal circumstances people would not have to dig out of the shambles left by darkness. They would not have to combat hunger, poverty, and despair. They would not be ruled by leaders who act only from self-interest and seek only to control others' lives in destructive and painful ways. They would not be suppressed and confused by religions and misled by religious leaders who know nothing about spiritual growth. Children would not be damaged by educational systems, and families would not perpetuate past life hurt and suffering. However, the darkness has done an excellent job and conditions are exceedingly far from ideal. In fact, conditions here are quite dark and evolution is extremely difficult, but not impossible.

In order for evolution to resume, souls must first regain control over the physical vehicles. Once this occurs, the voice of the soul can guide and direct the person toward situations and events that will provide necessary spiritual learning. Because each soul seeks to fulfill its own unique requirements, each soul seeks its own unique learning situations. Evolution is ultimately a process of returning to one's spiritual home.

Evolutionary requirements are earned somewhat like merit badges in boy scouts and girl scouts. The "badge," however, is more like a connection that is made in the consciousness between two points. It is necessary for each soul to make many, many connections. These connections are somewhat similar to an electrical wiring system. People could imagine that evolution is a process of seeking a higher vibration or state of existence. In order for a soul to sustain a higher energy, the consciousness must have adequate electrical wiring to support the current of each new vibration. When spiritual requirements are fulfilled, electrical connections can be made. When enough connections are made, the soul can sustain a more powerful energy or vibration. Only when the requirements are fulfilled can the connections be made. Only when the electrical system is adequate can the vibration be sustained.

Each human consciousness is unique. Each person makes connections in his or her own unique way, using the physical world to make these connections possible. These connections cannot be made, nor can a higher vibration be sustained, in environments that do not support evolution. People cannot remain in painful relationships and expect to evolve. They cannot maintain "comfortable," meaningless lives and expect to find enough opportunities to make connections and grow spiritually. They cannot misuse their sexual energy or work at jobs they hate and find evolution. Evolution only takes place in environments that are peaceful and with people who support spiritual growth. Many personal sacrifices must be made before evolution can occur. People must be willing to sacrifice their pain. Unfortunately, most people are not willing and have come to know the familiarity of their pain as a strange sort of comfort and friend.

INITIATIONS

Initiations are steps or stages in evolution. They are levels of existence, just like the levels in the animal kingdom. However, initiations are related only to the human soul. As souls gain higher vibrations and greater peace, they move up through these steps or stages. For the purpose of this book, humanity could think in terms of seven initiations. Every soul is destined to fulfill the requirements of these steps no matter how long that may take. In this sense, then, everyone is on a path of evolution. Some have chosen longer routes than others, but be assured that no path is an easy one. Each road has a price, a sacrifice that must be made. It is simply a question of whether humanity wishes to pay now and return home or pay later and return home.

At this time, 98 percent of the planet remains uninitiated and largely unaware of the fact that initiations even exist. It is the goal of the Brotherhood to bring as many souls as possible through the first initiation by the year 2000. The Brotherhood has established this goal because planetary energies are available at this time to make this goal a realistic possibility.

Each initiation is accomplished only after specific spiritual requirements are met. These requirements must be accomplished by the soul and could never be mastered through the human mind. Spiritual growth cannot be achieved in any other way. Physical world sacrifices are always required, but the reward for these sacrifices is beyond human comprehension.

Again, 98 percent of this planet has not yet achieved the soul vibration of a first degree initiate. The first initiation involves the sacrificing of the aggressive urges, of violence and of the emotional pain associated with uncontrolled impulses and desires. First degree initiates are beginning to understand the futility of being controlled by human desire and are beginning to see the hurtful, aggressive aspects of the human nature. They can stop themselves from using this energy against themselves or others because a piece of the human personality has surrendered to the soul.

Some souls have accomplished this by using the technology and information offered by the Brotherhood. These souls have simply made enough electrical connections to gain the first level of control over the human ego. Some souls have existed for a long time and have accidentally learned enough over thousands of years to fulfill the requirements of this first initiation. It is likely that these older souls have collected much misinformation and damage that will need to be healed before they can move on to the second step. Still others have accomplished this first step through some weekend workshop such as Erhard Seminar Training. Not all participants of such workshops accomplish spiritual growth. Most accomplish human ego growth. Those who do grow spiritually are burdened with a problem that the Brotherhood refers to as self-righteous positivism. These people are "positive" that they have their answers and are likely to wander for thousands of years with their "positive" approach because they simply cannot be reached by the Brotherhood. Many family members can attest to the fact that living with an EST graduate can be a very painful experience.

The second initiation is a refinement of the first. Here souls have learned to better control any leftover aggressions and to see the need for controlling emotional aggression as well as physical impulse. It is here that painful relationships built on mismanaged emotional aggression must be sacrificed. Souls must begin to obtain information about the physical world that will cause the connections in the consciousness necessary for the holding of higher vibrations. At the second initiation, people may need to learn about woodworking, welding, auto mechanics, plumbing or electrical wiring. They may need other information about relationships, computers or photography that will allow the soul to make the connections required to sustain a higher vibration.

Most second degree initiates, at this time, have obtained this level only after lifetimes of accidental learning, so they too are burdened with past life misinformation and damage. Very few souls have been able to accomplish evolution without creating other problems for themselves. For instance, because second degree initiates have a certain mastery over aspects of the physical world, they are often the comfortable ones—the ones who want convenient lives. They often will not sacrifice this comfort to move to the third level because they have spent so many hundreds or even thousands of years sustaining human comfort. They have used the will to stop any potentially growth-producing change.

The third degree initiate accomplishes this level only after specific requirements are met, requirements that may take thousands of years to master. These souls must have at least a limited mastery over certain aspects of the physical plane. They must have accomplished greater refinement of the first and second levels.

The third initiation involves opening the heart. Up to this point, people see the world only through the mind. They attract relationships based on their ideas of a marriage partner or friend rather than attracting people who will love them and support them. At the third initiation, people must look out at the world and see the heartache and human suffering that exists here. This is always a very painful experience.

Often, third degree initiates have had to fight their way to this level of spiritual growth. They have had to break from tradition and become individualists in order to reach spiritual achievement in a world that places no value on spiritual growth. They are often fiercely independent and are very attached to their independence. They are not easily moved to the next level.

The third level is probably the most dangerous and difficult stage of all the evolutionary steps. This aspect of growth will be discussed later in this work. Let us say for now that the third initiation can take many thousands of years in this endarkened system and can leave a soul too burdened to continue growing.

At the fourth level of initiation, a soul breaks from the attachments of the physical world. There are very few souls who have achieved this level, in part because humanity is so preoccupied with obtaining or owning the physical world. Fourth degree initiates have gained a mastery over the physical world so that they feel a certain amount of control over the physical environment. They are often behind-the-scenes people who work at some trade or craft in an attempt to further perfect their mastery. However, those few who do exist on this planet have reached this level only after nearly impossible sacrifices and lifetimes of difficulty.

Fifth, sixth, and seventh degree initiates seek only perfection in some form. Their requirements are, for the most part, not within the comprehension of those who might read this book. In fact, it would be safe to say that anyone reading this information who believes he or she is a fifth degree initiate or higher should probably stop right here. If you are a fifth degree initiate then the Brotherhood assures you that you do not need this information. If you are not a fifth degree initiate and believe that you are, you are too out of touch with reality to benefit from this work at this time. The Brotherhood recommends that you put this book down until you can recontact reality.

SOUL INFORMATION

At this point, we must reemphasize the fact that evolution is only accomplished under the direction of the soul. Spiritual growth cannot be achieved by expanding the human ego or improving the human personality. It would be foolish to think that evolution could be accomplished through psychotherapy or religion. It would be equally foolish to think that evolution would automatically be accomplished by making a bowl on a wood lathe or taking a course in electronics. It is true that spiritual requirements must be met before one can achieve a certain level of initiation. It is also true that many of these requirements involve certain skills in the physical world. But each soul has his or her own specific path for achieving these requirements and for making certain connections. Further, these connections must be made according to the timing of the soul, not the human ego. So, to think that one would automatically accomplish spiritual growth by signing up for a woodworking course would be foolish and short-sighted indeed. However, one would be more likely to remain less damaged and more prone to evolution by taking a woodworking course than by attending modern-day psychotherapy sessions.

There are those who would read this information and want to find out "where" they are in evolution. Although it is normal for human beings to be curious, receiving this information would lead most human personalities away from evolution. This information would cause some to see themselves as above others. For others, this information would cause them to see themselves as below others. Neither position produces healthy results. Some would imagine themselves as having occult powers. Others would think of themselves as privileged in a way that would cause them to stop being vigilant and responsible. The Brotherhood refers to these people as "legends in their own minds," and has unfortunately seen far too many "legends."

The Brotherhood is willing to offer humanity the necessary information to promote evolution. In addition to the technology briefly described in this chapter, the Brotherhood offers individual soul readings. Soul readings contain specific information that allows a person to know exactly what it is necessary to do if evolution is to continue. Soul readings are not meant to be psychic readings. The Brotherhood does not ever offer psychic information. Psychic information is obtained, for the most part, from souls who are themselves uninitiated and ignorant, who abide on the astral planes and know nothing about evolution.

Some psychic information is actually accurate. It is easy to understand why so many people are willing to pay so much money for an astral view of their lives. However, such a view, though somewhat sensational perhaps, produces no spiritual results whatsoever. People can be assured that 98 to 100 percent of current psychic information is absolutely useless as far as souls are concerned. Some of this information, even accurate information, is grossly misleading and may actually cause a person to stop growing spiritually.

Information from the Brotherhood is obtained from the Causal Field where genuine spiritual information exists. The information from the Brotherhood is channelled through telepathic communication to people who have made the necessary sacrifices and earned the right to receive such information. Very few, if any, psychics have earned the right to receive information from the Brotherhood.

The Brotherhood does not charge money for their healing instruments and soul readings. People can be asked to financially support the work of the Brotherhood if they feel they have been helped, but they can never be asked to pay fees. Humanity can be sure that the Brotherhood has no interest in earning a large income from the damages of people. Psychics who charge fees, particularly large, set fees, are absolutely not connected to the Brotherhood.

Soul readings offered by the Brotherhood are and will be much less desirable than psychic information because the Brotherhood is not attempting to please or appeal to the human ego in any way. People will say soul readings are not long enough, however the Brotherhood is not interested in burdening the human mind with useless information. They will say the Brotherhood is not "specific" enough because "specific" means the Brotherhood did not say what the individual "specifically" wanted to hear. The Brotherhood will tell each person exactly what they need to hear, but rarely will someone be told what they want to hear.

The Brotherhood provides soul readings because humanity has lost the ability to hear the voice of the soul. There is too much damage, too much noise for souls to get through and be heard. Soul readings give people only the information necessary to aid in a person's evolution. In a way, the Brotherhood is offering to speak to each person on behalf of the person's own soul. The Brotherhood simply tells a person what his or her own soul would be saying if that soul's voice could be heard. Certainly people can grow and evolve without the technology and information offered to humanity by the Brotherhood. The growth, however, would be slow, tedious and very difficult even for those strongly inclined toward spiritual growth. The Brotherhood is here to make evolution more simple, efficient and peaceful. This technology and the soul readings can eliminate thousands of years of useless suffering and haphazard attempts at spiritual growth.

The Brotherhood warns that there are many psychic, telepathic people who claim to be "channelling" information from the Brotherhood. There are many frauds, charlatans and fakes who think that evolution can be accomplished through the human mind, without sacrifices and without genuine healing of past hurts. This is not so. Very few people on this planet who claim to be connected to the Brotherhood are actually working with the Brotherhood in any way.

Humanity must find the truth in the midst of the New Age fads and false claims. People can only accomplish this by looking into themselves and judging this information from the heart, not the mind. People must discover evolution through the heart, not the mind. Soul readings must be approached from the heart, not the mind. This book is offered only as a guideline to those undertaking such a heartfelt search for what is real and true. Instructions for obtaining individual soul readings can be found in the Preface to this book.

☰

2

THE SEARCH FOR SPIRITUAL GROWTH

TODAY, PROBABLY MORE than ever before, people are searching for something "spiritual." They have looked everywhere except to their own souls and to the real spiritual leaders of this planet. Some have looked toward religion and found nothing but darkness, cloaked in meaningless rituals. Some have journeyed to the mountains and villages of India and found nothing but poverty and decay. Others have become so addicted to the search itself that they have forgotten what they were looking for in the first place.

Humanity will not find its true spiritual leaders here in the physical world. They will not find them in physical bodies. The spiritual world is a world of spirits—not ghosts, but highly evolved souls that comprise our planetary government known as Planetary Hierarchy. Planetary Hierarchy is like a spiritual ladder leading to higher states of consciousness. Hierarchy is not infinite but it is indefinite, which means that human minds cannot comprehend how far upward the ladder really goes. It is sufficient to think of Hierarchy as a group of highly advanced souls who direct and support the evolutionary process on this planet. The Brotherhood is a group of souls who both represent Hierarchy and act under the guidance of Hierarchy to work toward the spiritual betterment of this planet.

Although Planetary Hierarchy exists in the nonphysical world, there are many representations of Hierarchy in the physical world. Human representations of Hierarchy are generally irresponsible distortions of the Inner World system of government. For example, in the outer world certain people are respected as royalty. There are "royal couples" and "royal leaders." However, these so-called royal people do not devote their lives to any kind of spiritual leadership. They live in glamour and self-importance. They often have very little regard for the people they claim to represent. Human kings and queens are primarily interested in power, wealth and glamour. They refuse to see the plight of humanity and the suffering of their people.

Planetary Hierarchy has no interest other than the well-being of humanity. They have no need for physical world glamour, power or success because they live in a genuine spiritual world. They are completely opposite from human princes and princesses. In fact, they view all of humanity as royal kings and queens. Planetary Hierarchy thinks only of humanity and obtains no personal gain. These are our spiritual leaders. They offer no rituals, no religions, only evolution, ongoing spiritual growth governed by the spiritual laws of this planet.

People can think or believe anything they want about Planetary Hierarchy, but one day each soul is destined to see that Hierarchy is the salvation of humanity. The ladder that offers souls release from this planet is the ladder of Hierarchy. There is only one way out. Souls must evolve upward through the stages or initiations dictated by spiritual law. They are free to take as long as they want. However, there is still only one ladder, one Hierarchy and one Plan for the evolution of this planet.

Many, if not most people have held to some kind of religious faith at one time or another. Some still look to religion for spiritual guidance and support. Many people are aware that their search has been fruitless and even hurtful to themselves, but they continue anyway because they simply do not know where else to look. Many have developed strong ideas about spiritual growth, ideas that only reflect inaccurate religious doctrine and have nothing to do with real spiritual growth. For some, these incorrect ideas will prevent them from evolving again for hundreds and even thousands of years.

Many people are looking for God. They do not understand that religious ideas of God are incorrect and misleading, and that religions—all religions—were formed in darkness. All religions are meant to be misleading and are designed to prevent individual souls from obtaining accurate information. People are on this planet to build substance in their souls. Religion fails to provide even the basic information and tools to accomplish this task. Some religions have convinced people that there is no need to build; no need to be responsible for their lives, their relationships, or their souls.

People must understand that there is no heaven or hell as they imagine it. There is not even a god as they would envision him or her. There is a soul who is responsible for the evolution of this planet. This soul is the Planetary Logos. The Logos is the soul who embodies the planet earth and is probably the closest spiritual reality to human ideas of god. The Logos guides and directs the Plan of Evolution. He does not punish people nor can he hear anyone's prayers. There is much too great a gap between the vibration of humanity and the vibration of the Logos.

This does not mean he is without understanding for humanity. He is more compassionate and understanding of the human condition than anyone reading this could possibly imagine. Humanity lacks compassion. Humanity lacks understanding. The Logos lacks nothing. People must understand that their prayers, as humanity knows them, are almost always unheard, because prayer does not produce spiritual growth. Prayer is a mental exercise. People usually pray for their own human success, health, or happiness but not for spiritual growth. Planetary Hierarchy has no interest in human success and therefore has no connection to what humanity calls prayer.

People can connect with the Brotherhood. They can sincerely ask for support that would aid the evolution of their souls. The aid they would receive would be exactly what was needed for the accomplishment of individual evolution. People are and will be disappointed in this aid because they will get what they need, not what they want. When people begin to seek what they truly need, their prayers will be answered.

Religions have not taught people to seek what they need for

evolution. Religions have failed to provide spiritual leadership. They are outgrowths of darkness, founded on human pain and suffering.

CATHOLICISM

The Catholic religion is built upon a foundation of grandiosity. Grandiosity in its simplest form is the idea that people can act and do whatever they would feel like doing and expect eternal rewards for their actions, regardless of the effect of those actions on other people. Grandiosity is the idea that something is more important than it actually is. The Catholic Church attracts people who believe they are more important than they actually are. The Bishops, Cardinals and the Pope all think they have spiritual connections that they simply do not have. They thrive on self-importance. The Catholic Church thrives on self-importance. Their self-importance is reflected in the clothing, the jewels, the crowns and the robes. All of these are symbols of royalty worn, in this case, by people who have no spiritual royalty whatsoever. They have acquired these garments through self-righteousness and self-importance, not through any spiritual accomplishment.

The ministers of this religion believe they are better than other people. They literally look down on other people from their altars. The idea that priests are representative in some way of God or Christ is a foolish idea. The ministers of this religion all suffer from damages that are covered over with made-up ideas of self-importance. If one were to look into the private lives of priests, one would see them looking down on one another, or on those who tend to their homes, clean their houses and cook their meals. They expect to have their needs catered to without any reciprocity at all. They know nothing of healthy relationships. They have no compassion for people because they are too busy looking down on people. They believe they can get away with these things because they are doing so in the name of "God."

Catholic priests do not see that most of what they do is generated out of their own unresolved pathology and disturbance. If one were to look into their private lives one would find very serious problems and great disturbances, particularly in their relationships with their mothers. Priests, in general, are born into families with strongly controlling mothers. These mothers use their power over their sons to direct them into the priesthood. If their sons become priests, the mothers feel they have done their spiritual duty and have earned their "ticket" into heaven. These mothers are often under the illusion that they themselves are doing the right thing. They think they can manipulate the life of another person, and even severely damage that person, as long as they are doing it in the name of God. These mothers believe, as do most Catholics, that they can do anything to their children in the name of God because they think they are so important and so above other people.

These mothers have no regard for the individual needs of their sons. They have no concern for what their children's souls might actually be here to do. In general, they program their sons as one would program a computer. They reward "priest-like" behaviors such as loneliness, aloofness, and separateness. They convince themselves that they are making a biblical sort of sacrifice. These mothers do not foster healthy male-female relationships, laying instead the groundwork for celibacy. Many of these young men are vulnerable and cannot escape these early childhood impressions branded on the consciousness.

The priests grow up to act out their mothers' damages. They assume positions that give them the ability to control and manipulate other people's lives in the name of God. Priests know nothing of souls. They know nothing of spiritual growth. They know nothing of compassion. They know only what they have been taught by their mothers' damages. They know how to use unbridled self-importance to control other people and to lead them away from all possibility of spiritual growth.

The idea of celibacy is only perpetuated so that Catholic clergy can continue the illusion that they are above it all. Priests can think of themselves as above ministers, rabbis or any other clergy. Celibacy allows some priests to deny their humanity, their sexuality, their human needs and wants. It allows others to remain priests while secretly misusing women—often in their own parishes—for sex, while remaining detached from any human commitments and responsibilities. Very few clergy are prepared to relate in any normal, healthy way. Many misuse alcohol and suffer great depression and loneliness, conditions that have absolutely no spiritual value.

Those who participate in the Catholic Church are victims of their own grandiosity. Some actually believe they have been chosen above other people in order to follow the one true religion. No religion is based on truth. All present day religions are based on lies. Catholicism is founded on lies, damages and misinformation. Catholicism is built upon self-righteousness and contempt.

The ultimate grandiose idea is the notion of the plenary indulgence—the idea that a person could automatically gain the right to heaven by attending certain rituals or repeating so-called prayers. People who believe this idea usually think this gives them the right to emotionally abuse their children, their spouses and friends without any repercussions for such behaviors. People who believe this use self-importance to cover their own personal hurt and pain.

These and other ideas are strongly held in Catholic minds, often long after people have stopped attending formal Sunday services. Many of these souls hold so tightly to these incorrect ideas that they carry these notions into the nonphysical planes at the time of death. These souls are looking for "heaven," which they feel they have earned in spite of the unhealthy lives they have led. "Heaven," as they imagine it, does not exist. Yet, they insist they should be going to heaven. They refuse the help of the Brotherhood. They refuse to go to the places in the Inner World where they can be taught about evolution and healed of some pain. Their self-righteous insistence on "heaven" has caused these souls to get caught in the lower astral planes. Catholics might think of these planes as a kind of purgatory, but these places are hopeless, empty and very frightening. These places are difficult to get out of because they are so filled with people who have incorrect ideas. There is nothing but the chaos and confusion that results from incorrect ideas. These places are like cities with no doors.

Every day the Brotherhood attempts to work with souls that are caught out on these astral planes. The former Catholics are the least receptive to help and the most insistent on being granted heaven. The Brotherhood attempts to teach these souls of the need for evolution and the need to fulfill specific spiritual requirements. Catholics look at their score cards. They see their plenary indulgences. They see their rosaries, novenas and masses. The Brotherhood tries to teach them that their score cards have no value. People cannot live in hellish lives on earth and expect to find any kind of heaven. People cannot hurt and damage themselves and others and expect to walk into heaven.

Along with providing complete misinformation about the purpose of human existence, the Catholic Church controls the sexual energy of its members by preying upon their ignorance and fear. The "Church" frightens people into believing that by controlling their sexual energies throughout their adolescent and adult lives they will earn heaven and avoid hell. Such teachings prevent normal, healthy sexual relationships. Many Catholics are burdened as adults with unnecessary sexual problems, seeing themselves as bad or evil for having normal, healthy sexual needs and feelings. The priests are the ones who are unhealthy. They are the ones who fail to relate in healthy ways. Yet, they are the leaders of this religion and therefore are allowed to pass on their problems to the parishioners who seek their so-called guidance.

Many believe that the Pope is in some way God's representative on this planet. The Pope is the representative of darkness, of misused power and of disturbed illusions of self-importance. Rome is the seat of darkness. It is literally an area that is very black when seen from the Inner World. It is black because the papacy is built on lies. The Pope pretends to be a kind of a king. He wears his royal white robes. He visits countries of the world like a touring monarch. He looks at the faces of millions of poor, starving people, despondent people, every year. He lives in personal wealth. He offers nothing to alleviate poverty. He offers no real hope to despondent souls. He thinks that his presence alone actually helps people feel better. He parades through poverty-stricken nations and leaves all the poverty and pain in place, offering no relief. He knows nothing of human needs and of the emotional pain Catholics are suffering. He does not come to a nation to hear the problems of the people or to help build solutions. He comes to "offer" mass and to "grace" the people with his presence, to wave, and to give his so-called blessing.

The Pope has no interest in spiritual growth. He is only interested in rituals that cause him to feel important and in religious teachings that completely prevent evolution. He dresses in white. He pretends to offer hope. He gives lip-service to human pain and sorrow. He lives in wealth while many of his followers starve everyday. He is so seriously disturbed by his own delusions of self-importance that he thinks he is acting on behalf of God. He is not. He is only representing his own grandiose, self-righteous positions which have nothing to do with spiritual evolution whatsoever.

PROTESTANTISM

The Protestant religion is built upon self-righteousness and attracts self-righteous, narrow-minded people who pretend to be liberal and open-minded. The founders of Protestantism were "protesting" the grandiosity of the Catholics. These protesters believed that they had better ideas and approaches to God, better than the Pope and other Catholic leaders. The original Protestants actually believed they were rebelling against rigidity. They did not see that they themselves were as rigid and self-righteous as the teachings and leaders they were protesting against. Baptists, Methodists, Lutherans, and those of other Protestant denominations are all narrow-minded, rigid thinkers who have simply developed more rigid, incorrect ideas in the name of opposing incorrect ideas. What they opposed was the power and the suppression of the Catholic Church leaders—not because they knew it was based in darkness, but because they wanted some of the same power for themselves. One cannot fight against darkness with more darkness and expect to find the light.

Protestants believe that the Catholics are wrong and that the Protestants are right. They believe that their own made-up versions of religion extracted from the Bible will actually aid them spiritually. Protestantism is a religion of ideas—ideas that keep people in their minds and prevent them from looking at the pain and suffering in their lives. Protestant ideas are still energetically charged with the notion that these ideas combat evil and prevent darkness. Religious ideas are darkness. Protestantism is darkness cloaked in self-righteousness.

Protestants pride themselves on their hard work. They believe that if a person works hard enough, heaven can be achieved. Protestants do not see that people can work very hard at the wrong thing and cause no evolution or spiritual achievement. Protestants are taught to work hard at incorrect marriage relationships and incorrect jobs. They know nothing of what is required of souls. They know nothing of the actual hard work required if evolution is to be achieved. They only know of their self-righteous positions and their ideas that they are better because they work harder.

Protestants believe they can find their answers in the Bible. What they do not understand is that evolution cannot be accomplished through any book, not even the Bible. The Bible contains human interpretations of an inspired work. Without the help of the Brotherhood, people cannot determine the accurate from the inaccurate human interpretations. No more than one percent of all clergy has any connection to the Brotherhood. It is safe to say that, with very few exceptions, there are no Protestant ministers connected to the Brotherhood.

Protestants are actually protesting on the outside everything they do not want to look at on the inside. They refuse to look at their marriage relationships. They refuse to see what they might be doing with their children. They think that people can grow spiritually through the mind. They live in a world of ideas, and refuse to look at anything with their hearts. They live with overidealized thought-forms of marriage and family. They pretend that they provide proper parenting to their children, when in reality all they provide are self-righteous, rigid ideas of parenting. They establish their ideas of love and ideas of relating, but they know nothing of love, nothing of relating. One cannot love with one's mind. One cannot relate with one's mind.

Protestantism teaches people to project their personal problems outside of themselves. It teaches people to take self-righteous positions where other human beings are concerned. Protestants are taught to be petty and critical of others and even of one another. If one were to listen to the conversations at a Protestant social event, one would hear streams of critical, pejorative gossip. One would not hear Protestant Church members discussing their personal problems and hardships. Protestants deny their own problems. They deny their own darkness. They do not see that evolution can only be accomplished when people are willing to face their problems and reclaim the darkness for something better.

Protestants are protesting many things but they are not protesting the lack of spiritual growth on this planet today. Protestantism attracts people who think of themselves as being better than others; people who use their financial resources to build images and illusions of themselves as being better than others; people who believe that if they work hard and earn a sizable income, they have the right to do anything they want with that income. Protestants do not look at the planetary obligations to help others. They know only that they have worked hard and deserve a life of comfort in spite of the fact that their planetary neighbors are starving and homeless.

Protestants see themselves as "good," always good. They will not look at the parts of themselves that are self-righteous and narrow. They will not look at their own human selfishness and hurt. They wish to remain above it all. They refuse to admit to their passions, so consequently they are controlled by their own passions and desires.

Protestants believe they can be saved through Jesus Christ. They do not understand that Jesus Christ has no power to save them. They must save themselves by acknowledging their own darknesses, by looking within themselves. However, Protestants are unwilling to look within themselves. They are too busy working hard at all the wrong things in order to insure their own personal comfort. They are too busy searching the Bible for more self-righteous ideas with which to fill their minds. Evolution cannot be accomplished in any of the ways that Protestantism would proclaim. The Great Way is a road only traveled with an open heart, a generous spirit and a dedication to reclaim one's own personal hurts and sufferings. Protestantism teaches none of these principles.

JUDAISM

Judaism is built on separations. These separations are not spiritual. They are simply a reflection of the damages of the founders of Judaism. The Jewish people want to believe that God founded Judaism. Like all other religions, human beings founded Judaism— human beings who suffered severe damages that caused splits and fractures in the consciousness of the founders, splits that are now reflected in hundreds of separations throughout the Jewish religion and culture.

Within the orthodox system, women are separated from men and are considered unworthy of actual participation in the services. Women deserve only to observe the ritual. Although women are considered unequal and unworthy, Jewish women tend to compensate for this damaging system by placing themselves "above" it all. In some temples, women actually sit above it all, looking down on their men. There are many tasteless jokes about Jewish American princesses and Jewish women in general that express their obvious compensations.

The men are considered the ones who can think, read and understand. The men fill their minds with linear material and enter professions such as law and medicine. Ironically, for all their studying, they know very little about the physical world and are often incapable of even simple handyman tasks. Jewish women, for the most part, view men as incompetent little boys. The results of these positions are devastating to healthy human relationships.

The Jewish religion separates husbands and wives, fathers and daughters, brothers and sisters, mothers and sons. This separation causes problems in the male-female polarities. Men become passive, filled with meaningless mental junk. Women become "smarter" than men, controlling and dominating the family system from the masculine polarity.

The foundation of healthy human relationships is in the formation of a correct balance of the male and female sides of each person. When the balance breaks down as it has among most Jewish men and women, healthy relating breaks down as well. Jewish men and women suffer much isolation and loneliness in their relationships because they are simply unable to relate. Jewish couples learn to coexist. They remain detached. They are so accustomed to living in isolation that many would initially protest this information. However, few will find this inaccurate if they look closely at their lives.

Jewish children observe this loneliness. They feel it and accept it because they view loneliness as normal, and accept isolation and non-relating as signs of a stable, loving home. Because Jews are taught to see themselves as separate from and better than other people, they tend to marry their "own kind," so to speak. The tragedy is that the children tend to grow up and marry others like themselves who cannot relate. They then have children and the endless cycle of separation is carried on generation after generation without relief.

Jewish families live without any real emotional involvement. They thrive on mental involvement which allows them to remain detached and separated from one another. They remain detached from one another's pain and suffering. They make excellent lawyers and physicians because they are so detached and separated from the pain of their clients. They are satisfied to earn large salaries from the pain of their clients without relating to any form of human suffering.

Jewish people separate themselves from others. They separate their foods. They separate their dishes. They follow the Jewish calendar and celebrate many separate holidays. They build separate hospitals for their sick and separate rest homes for their aging. Some live in separate neighborhoods and attend separate Hebrew schools. However, these separations are only symbols of damage—damage that originated in the religion's founders and can now be found in over 85 percent of the world's Jewish population.

If these damages were healed, many Jews who now practice law and medicine simply would be unable to continue. They would be forced to relate to the pain and suffering of their clients. They would not want to face with an open heart those things they now suppress with the use of their linear minds.

These damages manifest in the Jewish people's search for a homeland. They wander because they have established themselves as separate. They feel "homeless" even when they have homes because they hold so strongly to the idea of being separate from others. They remain separate from their neighbors and separate from correctly relating to the physical world. Jewish men believe it is beneath them to become carpenters, electricians, welders. They aspire to become lawyers, dentists, physicians—all professions of the mind. They do not use their hands. They do not develop practical skills. They hire people to perform these services—people they consider to be beneath them. They do not connect to their homes in any physical way. They do not paint or repair their homes. They do not fix broken plumbing or faulty wiring. Many are incapable of relating to their homes in these ways. As a result, they have no real connection to their homes. They refuse to build, to establish for themselves. They remain separate and suffer an inner kind of homelessness no matter where they are.

Judaism is built upon damage and therefore offers nothing but damage. It offers no spiritual growth, no opportunities for making the connections necessary for growth. Members of the Jewish religion do not relate to one another or anybody else. Worst of all, they carry individual separateness from their own souls. They have used their human minds to rob their souls of any possibility of spiritual growth.

NEW AGE RELIGIONS

Over the years, some people have become dissatisfied with traditional versions of Catholicism, Protestantism and other religions.

Out of their discontent, they have formed groups such as the Unitarian Society, the Charismatics and the Born Again Christians. Each of these groups, built on discontent, is merely a perverted, distorted version of the original religion. Each is composed of people with exaggerated damages that magnetically draw them together. If these groups could see the darkness and blackness they have created by coming together and the damages they are passing among one another, they would be appalled at what they are calling "spiritual."

The Unitarian Society, although the least toxic, is founded on meaninglessness. It is composed of people who have no meaning in their lives and who have found no meaning in traditional religions. For the most part, we would say that Unitarians are experts in meaninglessness. They would not recognize genuine spiritual growth because they are only attracted to meaninglessness.

Unitarians read a vast array of meaningless books on New Age technologies and believe there are many "paths" to heaven. In a sense, they are correct. There are many "paths" to heaven, but there is only one Way—the Great Way. The Great Way is the road of purposefulness and meaningfulness. It is the one that can only be walked with an open heart. Unitarians avoid the Great Way and have managed to discover more meaningless paths than any single group on the planet. These paths are all traveled with the mind.

Unitarians pride themselves on being "open-minded." They are very open-minded and have managed to collect some of the most meaningless mental trash that this planet has to offer. They are not open-hearted. They are not seeking spiritual growth. They are seeking mental entertainment in a world of meaningless ideas. It is nearly impossible for the Brotherhood to work with any member of such a group. These people are so preoccupied and overburdened with their own personal ideas about spirituality and happiness that they cannot distinguish the Great Way. Their minds are too confused and their intellects too treasured to see the simplicity of genuine spiritual growth. The Unitarian Society is Western civilization's spiritual junkyard where old ideas that do not work can find a permanent home.

Unfortunately, these souls carry their baggages of misinformation with them even at death. Like the Catholics, they do not listen when their Inner World Brothers and Sisters attempt to bring them across the lower astral realms. They insist on remaining in places where they can continue the same lower mind ideas they had in physical life. The only places where souls can carry on this mental chaos are the lower astral planes—planes full of meaninglessness, aimlessness and confusion.

Charismatics are another group of those practicing New Age religion. They are the most psychologically disturbed of these groups and carry the most serious damages. These people actively wish to inflict their damages on one another. Some are women who use this group to become para-priests, exerting power and control over others in the group in the way that priests control and dominate their parishioners through exploitation and fear.

Many Charismatics believe they are so important that they are actually hearing Christ speak through them. Some of these people are hearing voices. However, the Brotherhood assures the Charismatics that they are not hearing the voice of Christ, a member of the Brotherhood. They are either hearing the echoes of their own disturbed minds or they have connected up with souls from the lower astral planes. Those who hear the voices of their own mind are mentally disturbed. Some would be hospitalized in psychiatric institutions if they were not actively acting out their pathologies at Charismatic meetings. They are experts at passing off their damages to vulnerable people who come to meetings seeking help. It is very dangerous, from the Brotherhood's vantage point, to seek help from a Charismatic group. One is far more likely to become further damaged by those claiming to hear the voice of Christ than to be helped in any way.

Those who are actually hearing voices are listening to desperate souls caught on the lower astral planes. The Inner World Brothers and Sisters observe these connections and can see that these Charismatics are taking their spiritual advice from desperate, lost souls— souls who have lived as alcoholics, criminals and back ward psychotics—very desperate souls who will do anything to find a way out of the lower astral planes.

Charismatics do nothing but damage one another in the name of Christ. These people act out their disturbances daily through telephone contacts and meetings. There is an urgency to attend services and meetings, to find new members and to make contact with old members. The energy behind this urgency is not spiritual ambition or a desire to serve. It is the urgency in members to continue to pass off disturbances and problems so they themselves will not have to face these problems.

There is no spiritual growth occurring in any Charismatic group anywhere on this planet. Spiritual growth cannot occur in environments of darkness and mental turbulence. Charismatics offer nothing but damage to individual souls and an opportunity for people to continue hurting themselves.

Finally, there are the Born Again Christians, who claim to have found the way to follow Jesus Christ. They do not even know who Jesus was or is and are only following their own incorrect ideas. Jesus came to this planet as a third degree initiate. Considering the fact that 98 percent of this planet is uninitiated, a third degree initiate is a relatively high vibration. Jesus came into incarnation so that he could accomplish the necessary spiritual requirements for the fourth initiation. Along with many other requirements, fourth degree initiates must break from the physical world. Jesus accomplished this through a sacrificial death. He did not come here to start a religion. He did not come to teach people to martyr themselves. He came to teach people about service to others and the need for continuous sacrifice on the road of evolution.

It is true that Jesus was given certain healing abilities by virtue of his level of initiation and his willingness to serve. There are a few people on this planet today who are genuine healers and actually have such abilities. There are many more who are fakes and charlatans who have no ability at all.

If Born Again Christians were truly followers of Jesus they would be seeking the information and technology necessary to fulfill evolutionary requirements. They would be much more interested in the simple, practical approach to individual soul growth than in sermons, songs and miracle healings. Jesus was an individual soul who diligently earned his vibration. He faced the great temptations of the human ego during his time on the desert. He used his free will to turn away from human wealth, power and glamour. He used spiritual will to accomplish evolutionary requirements. He used his time and energy to help the people around him.

Born Again Christians are not following Jesus in any way. They are as far away from his footprints as they could possibly get. They are not helping other people. They are not learning about real soul growth. They are too encumbered by their own ideas and dramatics to know anything about Jesus or evolution. They are only being born right back into purposelessness and darkness.

INDIA: THE SPIRITUAL BURIAL GROUND

There are many in the world who look to the East, particularly to India, for gurus and spiritual leaders. Some believe that India is a land of spiritual greatness. Yet, if they were to look closely, they would see a land of poverty, starvation and decay. They would see disease and hunger. They would not see spiritual wealth. They would see a kind of death, not a spiritual life force. Energetically, India might be looked at as a spiritual graveyard of old ideas and old ways.

Although there are a few fifth, sixth and seventh degree initiates on this planet, it is highly unlikely that anyone searching the mountains of India would be allowed near any initiates located there or anyplace else. Fifth, sixth and seventh degree initiates carry a vibration much too high to be subjected to the uninitiated. It would simply not be allowed.

People who search the East for gurus and masters would find as much spiritual wisdom in Detroit or Cincinnati as they would in most parts of India. People who travel in search of spiritual growth do not know the meaning of the word growth, because they have no investment at all in growing. They only have an investment in searching. If they were truly looking for growth they would see that it is impossible for most souls to grow amidst the stench, poverty and decay of India. Some people actually believe this poverty is some kind of spiritual simplicity. It is not. Hungry, starving people have no energy for growth. All of their resources are tied up in trying to accumulate enough food to stay alive. They have nothing left to use for evolution.

Most souls in India are lost souls who continue to be born into poverty and despair. Some worship cows and watch their children die of starvation. They have accepted despair and decay. They have no aspirations, no inspirations. They are too caught in the cycle of one empty, desperate lifetime after another.

Some of those seeking gurus believe they can grow by simply

being in the presence of someone with a higher vibration. Even if these seekers actually stumbled upon a higher level initiate, being in the presence of this initiate would not by itself be enough to accomplish growth. Unless a teacher can offer a technology that will heal the damages in the human consciousness, spiritual growth cannot be accomplished. Because Western society suffers from such a severe lack of spiritual leadership, people look to the East to find someone to follow. However, people do not see that the entire world is lacking in spiritual direction. Human beings look to other human beings to provide assistance and direction, but there are few true spiritual leaders living in physical bodies. Those who do exist on this planet are very well protected from the guru-seekers.

India has no spiritual leadership to offer. India is a country of darkness, hardship, pollution, and despair. This country is as spiritually bankrupt as a country could possibly be and has no resources to offer. India is a land where old religions and ideas die slowly away. Those who search for spiritual growth in India will find nothing but decaying philosophies and religious rubble.

THE FAILURE OF RELIGION

Religions have failed to provide for humanity. They have failed to provide spiritual leadership. They have failed to provide accurate spiritual information. Religions have failed to provide comfort for those who suffer. Most clergy know their teachings are failing. They know their people are suffering. Clergy members can feel the emptiness of their rituals and consolations when someone is dying. Clergy know that the people they are preaching to every Sunday have many unsolved problems and much unresolved hurt and pain. However, they like the illusions of power. Clergy like pretending that they are tending to their flock. They like the illusions of reverence and respect they receive from their congregations. They like their costumes and their special privileges. They like flying on clergy discounts. They like their special tables at their favorite restaurants. They like the special meals parishioners cook for them and they like vacationing in the summer homes of rich followers.

Church members are attracted to their religions because of their damages and the compensations for their damages. The Catholics suffer from their grandiosity; the Protestants from their self-righteousness; the Jews from their ideas of separation. Church members find comfort in the familiarity of their damages. Some people know they are doing nothing for their souls. Others know they have been duped, but are too proud to admit they have been "taken in" for so long. Some church members are bored and tired with weekly rituals that have no meaning. Some members know their church leaders are faking and that these so-called leaders have no healing ability, no spiritual nourishment, no real spiritual purpose. However, most people who belong to church groups are frightened and lost and caught in their damages. They are afraid of what will happen to them if they admit the truth to themselves. They fear there will be nothing to believe in and worry that they will not go to heaven when they die.

Church members will not find heaven at death because they have lived in lies and darkness in life. One cannot expect spiritual peace to come out of lives built on lies. One cannot expect to find a heavenly home in the Inner World by living out one's damages in the outer world. The clergy are false gods. Western church members would readily criticize the Hindu who worships the cow. While it is true that worshiping animals will not provide spiritual growth for one's soul, it is also true that souls cannot grow by worshiping false gods. Clergy are worse than cows. Cows do not pretend to be anything but cows. Clergy pretend to be spiritual representatives of God, while having no connection to the Logos or Planetary Hierarchy whatsoever.

Clergy pretend to offer spiritual information while they know nothing of what is required for an individual soul to achieve evolution. Clergy pretend to offer their church members comfort, but they have no ability to heal the damage and hurt of the people who come to them for aid. Cows do not pretend to know or do any of these things. Church members would be quick to criticize others but very slow to admit that their own emperors are very naked.

The Brotherhood of Inner World souls, guided by the Planetary Logos, offers humanity accurate and correct information about the purpose for humanity's existence. The Brotherhood offers the technology needed to heal the damages in the human consciousness. The Logos offers humanity the energies needed to accomplish individual soul evolution. The Brotherhood does not need discount air fares, special meals or vacation homes. They do not want to be worshiped. They only want souls to be returned to evolution. However, humanity is accustomed to worshiping false gods, cows, and anything else they can find to prevent themselves from achieving evolution. They are used to lies, illusions and gimmicks and will not expect to find genuine spiritual growth and real aid for their souls. At first, people will see the Brotherhood as just another religious hoax. They will not believe that the Brotherhood would offer healing instruments and soul readings without charge. People have had no experiences of genuine giving and true spiritual aid for real spiritual growth. Each person will need to discover for himself the presence of the Brotherhood and the nature of genuine spiritual growth, a discovery that cannot be made with the limited human mind but only through the heart.

3

THE SEARCH FOR RELIEF

THE EXPERTS

HUMANITY SUFFERS MUCH pain and sorrow. Souls ache for relief from past and present life damages. These damages perpetuate themselves by acting as magnetic points, attracting to themselves similar situations and events. Some souls, for example, caught in cycles of starvation and poverty simply continue to attract starvation and poverty for hundreds and even thousands of years. These souls are unable to grow because they must expend all of their energies and resources attempting to survive each day. Because they cannot grow, they cannot lift themselves out of the despair and darkness of poverty. More materially fortunate souls cannot yet see the spiritual importance of ending hunger and poverty. The materially fortunate ones are more interested in the glamour and personal attention they can receive for making any contribution to the cause of world hunger. Survival forms of relief will be discussed in later chapters.

Here, we wish to discuss what humanity might think of as psychological relief or emotional relief. As we have stated, damages in the human consciousness are held energetically in the etheric or light-weight body. These damages act as magnetic fields, not only for continuous cycles of poverty and despair, but also for chronic emotional pain and suffering. In Chapter One we discussed the example of Michael, who chronically attracted painful relationships that perpetuated his cycle of loss without resolution or growth. Souls are searching for something that will stop these chronic cycles of needless emotional pain. Unfortunately, people are not finding this relief because they are turning to people who cannot provide aid. They are asking for help from human beings who are suffering from the same chronic pain themselves.

Humanity looks toward psychiatry, psychology, social work, and counseling for "experts" on relief. People seek weekend workshops, "improvement" seminars and New Age technology for relief. Yet, souls have not found any relief. The people who claim to be healers and "experts" on relief suffer too much personal pain and damage themselves to provide anyone with real aid. These "experts" are like clergy members who pretend to offer spiritual assistance. Psychotherapists pretend to offer emotional assistance but instead they extend their own personal damages.

If humanity could see from the Brotherhood's point of view, they would not seek advice from these so-called experts. Humanity would see that these experts are some of the most severely damaged and disturbed people on this planet. Humanity would see that the "practice" of psychotherapy only offers these experts opportunities to disguise their own damages, or worse, to project these damages onto those seeking aid. If people looked carefully into the lives of psychiatrists and psychologists, they would see great disturbances. People would see that these "experts" have devastating personal relationships. They tend to project their damages onto their spouses and children just as they do with their patients. Psychiatrists and psychologists are experts at passing off and covering up their own personal damage. They enjoy comfortable incomes, prestige, and various forms of human success while offering absolutely nothing to alleviate damages to the human consciousness.

Psychotherapists offer nothing, or they offer damage, because they are not experts. People believe that experts can be established through higher education. People think that a college degree is a mark of achievement. This is not so. A college degree, at any level, is at best an indicator that a person has a good memory. At worst, and more often, it is simply a sign that a person has collected a large body of misinformation that will have to be untangled. Because people get so attached to incorrect ideas, the untangling process for some may take hundreds of years.

If a person aspires to be an electrician, that person must demonstrate that he or she has achieved the level of skill required to be licensed as an electrician. A master electrician is only certified when he or she has demonstrated certain abilities in the field of electricity. Most people would not knowingly seek an incompetent electrician to wire their home. Nor do local and state laws allow incompetent or unskilled electricians to "practice" their electrical skills until certification has been achieved.

When a person aspires to become a welder, that person must study and demonstrate his or her welding skills before certification can be achieved. People would not consider having welders build a highway bridge if they had only studied about welding in school. Local and state laws do not allow welders to construct bridges, nuclear power facilities, high-rise offices, or other buildings until specific levels of skill have been achieved.

Psychotherapists, on the other hand, are declared experts after "studying" about people in school and obtaining a college degree. This would not be such a travesty if what they had studied actually had something to do with providing relief to the human consciousness. What they have studied is inadequate and, to a great extent, incorrect information. So, psychotherapists are declared "experts" after studying vast amounts of misinformation which they then proceed to misuse.

Psychotherapists are not asked to demonstrate any level of skill whatsoever. They will claim that they become certified after a certain number of hours or years in practice. However, they do not become certified on the basis of consistently demonstrating their ability to provide genuine relief to the human consciousness. They become certified because they can recall the misinformation they memorized in school and apply that to a certification exam. Electricians must consistently demonstrate their ability to master electricity in all its practical forms. Welders must demonstrate their ability to weld consistently perfect joints. Psychotherapists are not asked to demonstrate any skill whatsoever.

Psychotherapists are not even asked to demonstrate their ability to manage their personal lives in healthy, competent ways. If humanity demanded that psychotherapists could continue to "practice" only if able to consistently demonstrate personal skill in the management of their own lives, there would be no declared experts. People would see that psychotherapists are too disturbed and damaged themselves to provide help to anyone else. They should not be called "doctor" and revered as experts any more than clergy should be called "reverend." Electricians and welders are masters of their trades. Psychotherapists are masters at disguising their damages, hiding their disturbances, and creating the illusion of the "expert."

THE PRACTICE OF PSYCHOTHERAPY

Many will claim they have been helped by psychotherapy. Some will even foolishly believe they are growing spiritually as a result of this professed help. People who cling to the idea that psychotherapy is valuable are attracted to incompetence and mediocrity. They know nothing about spiritual growth and they lack the imagination required to accomplish such growth. They believe that coping with their damages and trying to find comfort is all that life has to offer them.

Psychotherapy teaches people to cope with their psychological damages and to adjust into their pain. It teaches people to use their minds to compensate for their hurts and to build new illusions and behavior patterns that better protect the damage. Psychotherapy never removes the energetic sources of the damage itself.

Damage in the human consciousness is like a sore or wound that has not healed. If compared to a physical wound, this is the kind of emotional wound that might be filled with dirt and rocks and things that cause a great deal of pain. Worse, when the damage is left untreated, it begins to act like an infected wound. It attracts more of the same kind of negativity to itself and becomes a larger portion of a person's consciousness.

Psychological damages or wounds continue to become painful because they are often carried through lifetimes without proper healing and care. In order to function in a human consciousness, people erect protective behavior patterns that cover the damage.

People bandage or cover their psychological wounds with chronic negative behavior patterns. The behavior patterns, although negative, must be maintained in order to keep from experiencing the depth of hurt in the damage or wound itself.

When people seek psychotherapy, the chronic behavior patterns that are covering the sores in the consciousness have become painful in and of themselves. These chronic behavior patterns may even be breaking down, causing the original wound to be felt more poignantly. When people seek psychotherapy, they are looking for a way to reconstruct their protections. They have completely forgotten about the original damage and hurt because all their energies are tied up in protecting their wounds.

Psychotherapists themselves are wounded, but they have mastered chronic protective behavior patterns to a greater or lesser degree. They are not experts at providing relief, but they are very good at helping people reconstruct lies, illusions and negative behavior patterns that prevent the original damage or wound from being felt. When people claim to feel better as a result of psychotherapy they are simply saying they have made the necessary alterations in the human personality to keep their damages protected.

Some who attend psychotherapy have been further damaged by the experience. These "patients" are sometimes aware that they have been damaged but yet cannot stop the process. They are in too much pain and have no energy to fight. Those who are further damaged by psychotherapy are easy prey for those therapists who use their patients as dumping grounds for their own unresolved pain. Many psychotherapists have developed elaborate systems that allow them to pass their own damage to their patients. As long as they are able to project their problems out, they can prevent themselves from uncovering their own hurts and wounds. Psychotherapy, then, can be just another chronic negative behavior pattern for the psychotherapist, where the therapy itself acts as a protective bandage covering the therapist's own damage.

No matter what claims people may want to make about psychotherapy, it does not promote spiritual growth. In order for spiritual growth to be accomplished, people must be able to experience the guidance and direction of their own souls. They must be balanced and quiet inside so that the voice of the soul can be heard and followed.

When damages are present, the pain of the damage itself and the chronic protective behavior patterns are too loud for the soul to be heard. Protecting old hurts consumes enormous amounts of human energy. This energy must be unleashed in order for spiritual growth to occur. The soul needs the energy that is tied up in damages and behavior patterns.

Psychotherapists have no ability to alleviate the energetic sources of damage. They do not have the technology required to heal the human consciousness so that the voice of the soul can be heard. They have no ability to unlock the potential energy trapped in human suffering and pain. They therefore cannot restore a consciousness to a state of balance and peace where evolution could once again resume.

Psychotherapists are only capable of helping people protect their pain. As long as humanity's pain remains protected, humanity remains in darkness. Psychotherapists help people remain in darkness. And worse, the new lies and illusions that people erect through psychotherapy can take hundreds or even thousands of years to unravel. The new incorrect ideas accumulated through psychotherapy may take hundreds of years to correct. Those who claim that psychotherapy is of value have accumulated the biggest lies and the most misinformation. They are now invested in protecting psychotherapy, the very thing that taught them to protect their damage. The walls of protection are thicker than ever while the infection grows ever more painful underneath its covers. While their wounds fester, these advocates of psychotherapy are the least likely to seek the adequate, proper treatment now offered by the Brotherhood.

WHEN PSYCHOTHERAPY HEALS

In over 98 percent of all cases, psychotherapy provides absolutely no healing. Most can assume that their hours spent in psychotherapy have been fruitless and even destructive. However, it should be known that there are specific occasions, although extremely rare, when psychotherapy actually energetically produces a positive result. This result, which will be described later in this chapter, does not necessarily cause any evolution. However, it may lead a person to seek spiritual growth at some future time.

Humanity suffers from countless sources and kinds of psychological and emotional pain. People cover their pain with many chronic, empty behavior patterns. In many cases the pain and accompanying behavior patterns can be traced to a single devastating experience called alienation. People normally incur losses, hurts and sorrows as a result of being in incarnation. What makes these experiences so tragic is that most people have suffered their losses and hurts all alone, without any comfort or tending. It is the separation, isolation and lack of real emotional tending that make humanity's hurt run so deep. People simply do not feel camaraderie, kinship or any sense of belonging. They feel alone with their problems.

For example, if people were to look at American farmers in the 1980s, they would see families in great economic turmoil and distress. People would see hardship and loss, suicide, despair. Many farmers are losing their homes, their livelihood. No one comes to their aid. The American government provides no comfort or real aid because 50,000 farmers do not provide that many votes. Neighbors who could well afford to support and aid their fellow farmers watch and do nothing. They buy their so-called dearest friends' farm equipment at auction, offering no support, no comfort. America and most of humanity believe that "good fences make good neighbors," so most people do not make efforts to provide comfort to one another unless it is personally convenient.

People, particularly in Western society, can also look at their elderly who suffer emotional isolation and loneliness everyday. So much could be done to provide simple friendship and support. So little is offered that old age has become something to fear and dread.

Many souls have suffered losses similar to American farmers. Many souls have suffered isolation similar to Western society's elderly. Many souls carry the pain of these kinds of alienation.

Psychotherapy, under very specific conditions, can heal alienation. However, this occurs only when either the therapist or the patient is already healthy. Unfortunately, psychotherapists as a group are very unhealthy, with some 90 percent suffering from severe personal problems. The pathology of some psychotherapists is so severe that they might well become dysfunctional if they were unable to project their problems onto their clients on a continuous basis. So, most patients are seeking help from people who are too sick to help them.

When people seek psychotherapy, they are often in much inner pain. Patients are actually more likely to be healthy than psychotherapists, but still suffer many personal problems as a group.

Assuming that by some rare possibility either the therapist or patient is healthy, the second requirement for healing alienation is that they must be able to link up energetically in a way that produces the experience of kinship. This experience only occurs with the correct Sun, Saturn, and Mars connections in the two astrological charts. These exact connections are difficult to find. Neither patients nor psychotherapists would be able to determine these exact connections, even with a reasonable knowledge of present day astrology. Humanity has not yet earned the high level of astrological knowledge necessary to calculate these connections. Since psychotherapists are, for the most part, still dedicated to their personal pathologies, this astrological information cannot yet be given to humanity.

If a psychotherapist had clairvoyant vision and was directed or guided by a seventh degree initiate, this energetic combination could easily be accomplished. The clairvoyant vision would allow the therapist to see the color combinations and movement in the aura of the client as they blended with his or her own in a very specific way. In this energetic blending or chemistry, both the therapist and patient would experience a sense of kinship and belonging. This energetic experience of kinship and belonging would positively affect the hurts and wounds in the patient's consciousness, and, in some cases, would cause the energetic sources of these problems to begin to break up into the energy of belonging. This experience would not cause any linkage with the person's soul needed for evolution. It might, however, allow the person the opportunity to be released from chronic behavior patterns that were once needed to protect the wounds. Once released from chronic behavior patterns growth becomes a possibility, but is in no way insured.

Since today the "healers" are too sick themselves to be of any real aid, the likelihood of this process happening is extremely rare. When it has occurred, it has been by absolute accident. For those few who found kinship, the experience was unmistakable.

PROVIDING PSYCHOLOGICAL SUPPORT

Since providing an experience of kinship or of belonging is well outside the realm of most psychotherapists, any healing of the consciousness remains minimal or nonexistent. If psychotherapists were interested in providing certain psychological relief, they could provide a certain kind of human aid. This support would not affect the damages or provide healing to the overall consciousness, but it would be a much more positive use of the therapist's and patient's time and energy.

Again, to provide the human psychological aid to be described, the psychotherapists must want to provide something of value. This would mean that a therapist must be committed to healing his or her own consciousness, and actually looking at his or her own problems. Since psychotherapists are experts at "not looking" at themselves, they will probably not be interested in the following suggestions.

It would also mean that psychotherapists would have to develop compassion for humanity. This approach could interfere with their standard fees for service. Without their current set fees, many therapists would have to reconsider their present lives of comfort, convenience, and in some cases, personal wealth. Again, such reconsideration would be very unwelcomed by most of today's psychiatrists and psychologists who do not want to deal with the personal involvement necessary to develop human compassion.

However, for the sake of those few who would want to help in a limited way, the Brotherhood suggests that therapists work only with human worry. Everyone on this planet worries about something. Worry consumes much time and resources. It causes people to live unbalanced and distressing lives.

Worry is not necessarily related to damage in the consciousness. It is, for most people, just a normal functioning like breathing and eating, only much more distressing. A person's worries can generally be traced to the position of Saturn in the astrological chart. There are twelve areas of worry that correspond to the twelve astrological signs. This is not a perfect system, but it is accurate enough to offer a guideline to the interested therapist. These worries may manifest in many ways, but can usually be traced directly to the Saturn placement.

It should be understood that when a person's primary worry is activated or directly confronted, the automatic human response is one of false pride. In order to handle the human pride automatically triggered by confrontation of the worry, the therapist must approach each patient as though that person has extreme and great value. The therapist should feel about the client as one would feel about someone who has given great service. The therapist could imagine that the client once saved the therapist's life or the life of the therapist's child. The therapist must hold the client in high esteem and regard without any of the self-righteous belittling of clients normally done by psychotherapists. Again, very few therapists would hold their clients in high regard, although they might claim to do so.

Once human pride can be properly managed (it cannot be avoided), the therapist and client need to discuss their personal worries. Each could relate his or her own worries and begin to learn about when, where and how these worries manifest. This would not produce evolution of any kind, but it would be the beginning of people helping one another to understand the human condition and to manage the pitfalls of the human personality. These worries would never be analyzed nor would they be diagnosed. None of the present psychological systems of misinformation could be used.

Again, it is highly unlikely that any of today's psychotherapists could become healthy, develop compassion, stop charging set fees, treat their clients with dignity and respect, give up their misinformed ideas and actually want to help. However, for those few who do, the twelve major areas of worry are listed below. It is further suggested that any therapist interested in this information use the healing instruments developed by the Brotherhood for at least six months before undertaking this effort. These instruments can be obtained through Gentle Wind Retreat (see address in Preface).

SATURN PLACEMENT	KEY WORD	PRIMARY WORRY
Aries	Substance	Worries about not being full, whole, physically complete; worries about size and shape of body parts.

SATURN PLACEMENT	KEY WORD	PRIMARY WORRY
Taurus	Form	Worries about not having enough supplies, money, resources.
Gemini	Possibilities	Worries about not being able to figure things out; worries about losing control because he/she has not figured something or everything out.
Cancer	Needs	Worries about getting needs met.
Leo	Impulse	Worries about losing control of self, losing control of feelings, impulses.
Virgo	Assimilation	Worries about not being able to take in information; worries about not being able to learn.
Libra	Elimination	Worries about not being able to get rid of things he/she no longer wants or needs; ie: relationships.
Scorpio	Orientation	Worries about not fitting into groups and situations; worries that he/she will not find a place.
Sagittarius	Capacity	Worries that he/she will not be able to live up to the expectations of others; worries that he/she does not have what it takes to get a job done.
Capricorn	Charisma	Worries about not being appealing to people; worries about not being able to make it to the top.

SATURN PLACEMENT	KEY WORD	PRIMARY WORRY
Aquarius	Means	Worries about not finding a path in life or not having the means to do what he/she came here to do.
Pisces	Goals	Worries about not knowing where he/ she is going; worries about not knowing his/her needs; worries about not being able to see through own inner fog.

WORKSHOPS AND SEMINARS

In recent decades, people have turned to the idea of weekend work-shops, seminars and groups as sources of relief from their psychological pain and suffering. Again, people look toward darkness with the hope of finding light. Overall, these so-called experiences do not produce any spiritual growth. A few souls do find limited benefit through "EST" and "Insight," and a small number of other techniques. Unfortunately, those who do find benefit are also burdened with a whole new set of problems. These problems are extremely difficult to unravel and present very serious barriers to any further evolution. The Brotherhood, guided by the Planetary Logos, offers evolution without baggage—a far more simple and efficient way for souls to achieve much-needed spiritual growth.

Most of the current day workshops and seminars have been constructed to protect the leaders' damages. The leaders are often psychotherapists who are masters at protecting their damages. These psychotherapists developed workshops because they saw the opportunity to construct new illusions about themselves, and to also gain the added benefits of personal power, prestige, and financial gain. None of these seminars were constructed because someone saw the psychological pain of humanity and felt the need to provide relief. All were constructed out of damage.

For example, those workshops constructed by women to aid other women in "exploring" themselves are led by women who suffer serious personal problems with the female polarity. These leaders design seminars to teach other women to become more competitive, more aggressive, and masculine. They do not see that the competitive force is the force of war and power that has led this planet into a dangerous state of confusion. These "experts" exploit the damages of women suffering from chronic behavior patterns of worthlessness and helplessness. These patterns reflect the damage already incurred by previous misuse of the competitive force. Simply stated, neither powerfulness nor powerlessness can restore peace in the human consciousness and promote evolution of any kind.

Some people claim they have been helped by these experiences. Again, these claims are based on ignorance and genuine desire for incompetence and mediocrity. Those who claim they have been helped have undergone the same kind of personality and behavior alteration that psychotherapy provides. These people have simply found new chronic behavior patterns to protect the original sources of damage and pain. None of these leaders and so-called experts have designed a seminar that will energetically remove damage from the human consciousness. For the most part, these "experts" are not connected to the Brotherhood and do not have the skill or technology to alleviate damage. They simply help people become better adjusted to their damage by establishing a new set of lies and illusions that cover the damage.

Many of these seminars are engineered to cause people to get "high" and elated at their new illusions. Often these "highs" are accompanied by great lows in the weeks or months following the seminar. Participants also learn new, complicated ways of projecting their own problems onto other people, another skill common to their psychotherapist-leaders and workshop designers. Often these newly acquired projection skills cause further damage to the family members of workshop participants. The damage is often done in the name of sharing and honesty, leaving family members no recourse to ward off the projections.

Occasionally, but not very often, a few seminar participants accidently look at enough of their own problems to cause limited spiritual growth. These few participants may even move to the first or second levels of initiation by relinquishing enough of their aggressive nature to cause a lift in the soul vibration. However, they are not able to avoid the new protections offered for the purpose of covering damages that still remain in place. They therefore incur many barriers to future spiritual gain.

The Brotherhood terms the most common form of spiritual baggage "self-righteous positivism," which is incurred by most EST and Insight graduates. Self-righteous positivism causes people to believe they have found a correct spiritual path, which they have not. It causes them to be "positive" about what they know without leaving room for enough self-doubt and humility to see the possibility of another way. It causes people to develop a manipulative language system that always leaves the other person in the hot seat, while failing to face their own personal problems in any realistic way. Self-righteous positivism makes monsters out of even good people, as many family members of these seminar graduates would attest.

Finally, workshops and seminars that offer psychological growth through groups are like religions that offer spiritual growth to the masses. Neither understands the fact that each soul is here for a specific purpose. Each soul has its own unique destiny, requiring its own unique kinds of help and support. Spiritual growth occurs within the individual consciousness through the proper use of individual free will. It cannot be accomplished through a group experience or an experience in groupness. This is not to say that participants do not enjoy the much-needed affection offered at times in these groups. It is to say that souls cannot grow simply because someone has received much-welcomed affection. Further, it is a travesty to see how many people continue to pay $400, $600 or $1000 for affection because they have been unable to get support any other way.

NEW AGE TECHNIQUES

Many who feel that traditional psychotherapy has failed them now seek relief among the myriad of New Age techniques. These techniques, though in some cases more sensational and exotic than psychotherapy, do not offer spiritual growth of any kind. In fact, the New Age approaches are more dangerous than psychotherapy because many of them claim to be spiritual and uplifting when they are not.

New Age seekers have developed the idea that there are many paths and that New Age techniques such as meditation, psychic readings, astrology, "crystal" therapy, rebirthing, floating in isolation tanks, are all spiritual paths. These ideas are wrong. These approaches are no more spiritual than religion or psychotherapy. There is only one road of evolution and these New Age approaches do not lead to that road. If anything, they are all paths away from genuine spiritual growth.

Those who believe that evolution can be accomplished through meditation are seriously mistaken. Although most forms of meditation may be less harmful than other New Age approaches, they are not spiritual. Meditation may calm some of the human mind chatter and in that sense may even provide temporary human relief. Meditation, visualization, or any technique of the human mind cannot, however, heal damage in the human consciousness and connect a person to the soul. Evolution absolutely cannot be accomplished through the human mind. Spiritual growth can only be accomplished through the soul.

Some meditators claim that they become more detached from their problems. They are using meditation to ward off their problems and damages. They are simply using their minds to prevent themselves from facing their lives. So they actually are correct in their claims. They are more detached, but also further away from solving their problems than ever before.

A few meditators believe that by meditating in a group or in the presence of a Master, spiritual growth can be accomplished. If, in fact, someone had actually found a true Master, a seventh degree initiate, it might be possible to absorb the Master's vibration over a long period of time. The problem is that most people have not found Masters. They have found charlatans and fakes, or they have found second, third or fourth degree initiates who have broken from the path and are doing their own thing. Charlatans and renegade initiates have no vibration for anyone to absorb. If someone actually found a seventh degree initiate, the absorption process would take hundreds or even thousands of years, not a single lifetime. Even correct or useful forms of meditation under ideal conditions do not provide efficient means for evolution.

Some people believe that spiritual growth can be achieved through psychic readings. These people may even believe that the Brotherhood is working through their favorite psychics. The Brotherhood is not interested in psychic information—not even accurate psychic information. Psychic misinformation is obtained from impostors who have no psychic ability. Semi-accurate psychic information is received by psychics who have connected with souls on the lower astral planes. Often these souls are lost, desperate and ignorant. These souls are simply looking for a route back into incarnation and will do anything to acquire that route. Astral souls know nothing about evolution, which is why they are caught on the astral plane. They can read certain thoughts or patterns in a person's life. But these souls are incapable of telling people anything they do not already know. These astral souls have no access to the records of a person's soul where the necessary sacred data is stored. Accurate psychic information comes from the higher astral plane and may be offered by slightly more advanced souls. Accurate psychic information often satisfies human curiosity and dazzles the information seeker. However, this information, as accurate as it may be, has nothing to do with what the person's soul needs to know. Psychic information is always given for the satisfaction and entertainment of the human ego. It is never given to the soul.

Soul readings from the Brotherhood are obtained through telepathic channelling. They come only from the causal plane and never from the astral spheres. The Brotherhood is only interested in soul information, which does not often satisfy the curiosity of the human ego. Soul readings tell an individual soul exactly what that soul needs to hear in order to take the next step in evolution. Each soul needs specific information about what is required in order for that soul to accomplish spiritual growth. The Brotherhood does not work through psychics who want to be known as "psychics." Therefore, it is safe to assume that the Brotherhood is not working through any known psychic at this time.

Astrology could offer humanity accurate information about the human personality if astrology was a more accurate science. At present, astrology represents a small portion of accurate data and a large portion of interpretations which represent the damages of the interpreters. More astrological information will be available in future works. However, even accurate astrological information will only describe the human personality. It will not provide any information about what is required for the evolution of the soul.

Many New Age techniques have not only led people away from their souls but have actually caused damage to those who sought these so-called paths. The most damaging of all New Age technologies is walking on hot coals. Human beings were not designed to walk on hot coals. In order to walk on hot coals and stay inside the human consciousness, a person would have to experience extreme pain. With special instructions, however, people can be taught to split themselves off from their consciousness. By splitting off from their own damages, they can walk on hot coals without extreme pain. These people actually split themselves into energetic pieces. They damage themselves in a way that is extremely difficult to repair, even in the Inner World after physical death.

People who walk on hot coals do not seek to be repaired because they often like the "high." They like the split. They do not want to reclaim the damages. They do not see that a fractured consciousness remains in spiritual darkness and cannot possibly grow. They do not understand that evolution can only be accomplished by making energetic connections with one's own consciousness. These connections cannot be made until the splits and fractures are healed.

There are New Age breathing techniques that can produce enough pressure in the human consciousness to cause the same fracturing and splitting off of the damages. These techniques usually involve repetitive breathing patterns, sometimes while sitting in hot tubs. These breathing techniques often cause people to feel very high and elated. If people used these techniques a few times, very carefully, they could find limited relief from their human problems. They would not be healed, but in certain cases they would feel a temporary lift. But to most in humanity, "more is better," so they practice these fruitless exercises until they are split into separate energetic compartments. They continue to get "high," and they also continue to damage themselves, often so severely that they could only be healed through return to the Inner World at physical death.

There are literally thousands of self-proclaimed New Age paths. To discuss them all would be a fruitless endeavor, although perhaps entertaining to the seekers themselves. The Brotherhood and the Planetary Logos have no interest in entertaining technique seekers. Simply stated, none, absolutely none, of today's New Age techniques lead souls back to a path of spiritual repair and ongoing evolution. As exotic, glamourous, lucrative and sensational as these techniques may be, they simply do not work.

DRUGS, DIET AND EXERCISE

People, particularly in Western societies, have come to believe that evolution can be achieved by getting high on drugs, eating particular foods, or performing daily exercise. Getting high on drugs has nothing to do with increasing the vibration of one's soul. No drugs, not cocaine, LSD, marijuana, or "ecstasy," offer any avenue of spiritual growth, no matter how dramatic the effects of these drugs might be.

People who use drugs claim they have had new experiences of heightened awareness. They claim to see the light of truth about themselves and those around them. They claim to feel great release from their suffering, and believe they have reached altered states of consciousness. Some claim that they know God through drugs or that they have made contact with their one true source.

Drugs may induce hallucinations. They may cause unusual and even bizarre body sensations. They may give certain people access to the lower astral planes. Drugs may give certain temporary relief from pain by numbing the consciousness and altering normal thought patterns. Drugs do not produce spiritual growth. No one has ever made contact with the Planetary Logos through some drug induced experience. The source of each soul emanates from one of six celestial spheres that are not recontacted through the use of drugs.

People, particularly in Western society, have come to believe in quick fixes, easy money and fast food. They apply these reckless, irresponsible thinking patterns to spiritual growth. They delude themselves into believing that spiritual evolution can be accomplished by swallowing a pill. They fail to see that evolution is very difficult to accomplish and that spiritual growth requires hard work and personal sacrifice. They are blinded to the physical damages caused by certain drugs. They would be appalled to see the deadened brain cells and deteriorating digestive systems of those who regularly use "ecstasy" and proclaim its spiritual value.

The world of drugs is a world of illusions and emptiness. It is a world where sellers and manufacturers make money off of damaged, suffering souls. It is not a world dedicated to the peace and restoration of humanity.

Some people believe that evolution can be accomplished by eating certain foods or fasting. These people do not understand that the soul gives life force to the body. The body does not give life force to the soul. They believe that through some illusion of a "pure" body, one will achieve a pure soul. These people know nothing of their souls nor do they understand the needs of the physical body. Macrobiotics and other specialty diets are beneficial only to a very small portion of the human population. Even for these few people, specialty diets are beneficial only to the physical body, not the soul. In many cases, these diets actually produce malnutrition. These diets stress the physical vehicle and place unnecessary pressure on weakened or vulnerable organs and systems.

Some people believe that "fasting" (not eating or limited eating) is a spiritual experience. Fasting is usually deprivation and malnutrition. It is not a spiritual experience. Those who fast may feel elated and light-headed, and think that these early symptoms of malnutrition are actually spiritual events. They believe that people can purge the consciousness by starving the body. The human consciousness cannot be purged of its damage and darkness through starvation. Each person is responsible for the care and maintenance of his or her own physical body. Macrobiotic diets and fasting have extremely limited value even where proper physical maintenance is concerned. Again, neither fasting or a specialty diet ever produces anything that aids the consciousness or fuels the soul.

Throughout the Western world, people are caught in the glamourous ideas of physical appearance and the physical health benefits of exercise. Some even believe that exercise produces spiritual growth. There are groups who actually believe that combining meditation with running will produce results that can benefit the soul. Nothing could be further from the truth. These people think the "runner's high," produced by a lack of oxygen to brain cells, is a spiritual experience. They run beyond their physical capacities. Some run long distances for many hours. They do continuous damage to their bodies. They destroy their brain cells. Some are dangerously close to destroying cells required for normal human functioning. Their bodies are severely weakened by overexertion.

They waste energy needed by their souls for growth, while they do absolutely nothing to benefit their souls.

People can only evolve by looking at themselves, their darknesses, pain and suffering. They cannot evolve by literally attempting to run away from themselves. They are, more accurately, running themselves into the ground.

4

EDUCATION

THE PHYSICAL WORLD exists so that souls can accomplish evolutionary requirements. This means that the world is here as a potential
classroom for souls, where real learning can take place. However,
humanity does not use the physical world for evolution. In fact,
people use the physical world for almost everything but evolution.
People want to own things and to have control over others in the
world. They want to dominate and have power. They want to accumulate wealth and property. They want professional achievement
and the feeling of success. They attempt to find "happiness" in a
very unhappy place and they seek comfort and sameness in a world
designed to provide continuous change.

Humanity has lost the information and know-how necessary to
correctly utilize their own world. One of the greatest barriers to real
learning through proper use of the physical world is education.
Education, in all its forms, was instituted in darkness, and therefore
can do nothing except keep people in the dark. People, particularly
those in Western societies, make much of their educational systems.
They emphasize the idea of "getting a good education" and going

on to "higher" education. They do not understand that the more education people receive, the more they become disconnected from real learning.

Real learning about the physical world can only take place when a person is able to make certain connections about the world that correlate to connections in the human consciousness. Evolution occurs when people are able to link the human personality with the soul. This means that the human personality must be brought to a high enough state so that the soul can work through and guide the human consciousness. In order for this linking to take place, people must sacrifice their pain, hurt, incorrect relationships, misguided ideas, and chronic behavior patterns. They must also be able to connect certain pathways between the soul and the personality. Later, they must connect pathways between the soul and the spirit, the source of their own existence. These pathways and connections in the human consciousness all have their representations in the physical world. When people are able to learn certain skills and directly relate to the functioning of the physical world, they are able to make certain connections inside the consciousness necessary for evolution.

It should also be understood that connections or pathways can most efficiently be accomplished in a time sequence unique to each soul. Soul readings from the Brotherhood allow people to know what is required of them in order to accomplish their next steps in evolution. Without such information, evolution is mostly accidental. People now take thousands of years to make connections that could be done in a matter of years or even months because they simply do not have the correct information about learning in the physical world.

Education severely impedes spiritual growth and real learning by causing people to disconnect from the physical world and to overemphasize the human mental world. Children learn to read but they do not read books that connect them into the physical world. Schools teach children mathematics but do not apply those mathematical skills to building and creating things in the physical world. Children learn about geometry. But children do not learn how the angles of the chair they are sitting on must connect in order for the chair to safely provide a seat.

Schools claim to teach science but fail to educate children about why they are on this planet. Schools teach children about trees, providing them with all the scientific names, but children do not connect to the fact that wood is a vital part of construction within most societies. Children eat out of wooden bowls, write on wooden tables, use wooden pencils, yet they have no real connection to the fact that all these things were once trees.

Schools claim to teach children about electricity, but very few high school graduates can locate the fuse boxes in their homes. Even fewer could repair a fuse or reset a circuit breaker. Most children graduate from high school unable to fix a leaky faucet or to repair a broken toilet. The "brighter" the student, the less likely he or she is to have acquired any of these simple skills.

Real learning can only occur when proper connections are made. Education severs connections and actually causes people to disconnect from things they have already accomplished. Education blocks that normal curiosity of humanity which once impelled souls toward learning and connecting. It stifles the human creativity and self-expression essential for spiritual growth. It is a system of complete endarkenment based on memorization, not real learning. This system has singlehandedly caused more damage to humanity at large than religion or any other social or political system. It has left people without the understanding of where things come from and how they are made. Very few people comprehend the miracle of the car engine or the fact that simple motors are running in the refrigerator, the washer, the lawn mower and the vacuum cleaner. They do not know how electricity generates light, how oil becomes heat, or how water flows through home plumbing systems. The more educated a person becomes the less connected he or she is to the physical world, and the more disconnected from his or her own soul.

The system of education has actually caused energetic splits in people by consistently offering mental information that has no relationship to physical reality. This split is visible from the Inner World and found in the etheric web of many now in incarnation. The split inhibits learning, even under rare conditions where learning can take place. It causes an inability in people to properly integrate information into the consciousness. This split can be mended, but at this time it can only be done through the technology offered by the Brotherhood. There is simply no other equipment on the planet sophisticated enough to accomplish this repair.

LEARNING ENVIRONMENTS

Schools claim to be learning environments. They claim to offer students a place to learn. Yet education damages over 80 percent of the school population every year. The educational system is built on the idea that the way to learn is by not making any mistakes. Good students with good grades are rewarded because they do not make many mistakes. This type of student constitutes about 20 percent of the world population involved in formal education. This group of so-called good students usually includes only those people who have good linear memory systems. They can memorize the subjects offered to them even though these subjects have no meaning. The good students are trained, then, to memorize meaningless data and to compete throughout their schooling for academic standing. In the human sense these students experience a certain amount of success, and are not usually the target of their educators' disapproval or contempt. This 20 percent of the school population learns very little of any real value, but they do not incur the kinds of damages now seen in over 80 percent of humanity—damages that can be traced directly to the educational system.

Because the system rewards people who can memorize and avoid making mistakes, education punishes people when they do make mistakes. Education gives low grades, teacher disapproval and societal condemnation to people who make mistakes, causing these students to view themselves as failures. This negative view of the self is the cause of much human suffering. People carry this view of themselves as failures beyond their education, possibly becoming jobless or homeless as they continue to energize the false idea of personal failure. They turn away from new experiences and discount their own ability to learn. They hurt themselves inside, and carry the idea of personal failure into their relationships and home life.

Education has failed to provide a healthy environment where anybody and everybody can learn. It has failed 80 percent of the school population, who either do not learn through memory or are simply disinterested in the misinformation being taught. Education will not allow people to learn because it will not allow people to make mistakes. Learning requires a safe, supportive environment where mistakes are not only encouraged but are actually transformed into greater learning. People naturally make mistakes because they naturally want to learn. Education absolutely refuses to support learning.

Since education provides no opportunity to learn, it produces only darkness. Souls cannot make the necessary connections in a system that punishes mistakes and disapproves of 80 percent of the population. Moreover, each soul has a natural inclination to learn those things that will help fulfill its own purpose. Each soul has a natural curiosity and interest in subjects that support its individual soul destiny. Education cares nothing about the individual and knows nothing about soul destiny. The more connected the soul is to the human personality, the more a person will be inclined to reject the educational system for failing to provide relevant data.

Education not only creates failures, but treats people as though everyone is the same. Everyone generally takes the same subjects, reads the same irrelevant books and is graded according to the same condemning system. Yet each soul requires different learning at different times.

As a result, children who might be excellent readers are considered below grade level because they cannot connect to what is being offered as reading material. Children who might do well in mathematics reject it because no one has taken them to a woodworking shop where mathematics can be applied, providing them with real learning. School systems spend millions of dollars on updated learning programs designed for the masses, rather than looking more closely at the individual consciousness of each student and considering what might be required to produce learning and growth. Education is a narrow, linear, stagnant system that has no regard for the individual.

A few students enter the Industrial Arts program, where woodworking, welding, auto mechanics, and other such courses are taught. Unfortunately, these programs are generally unavailable to the large population, except as a short term course or elective in certain schools. Those who do attend "vocational" schools are usually labeled as rejects and failures who must use their hands because they are unwilling or unable to use their minds. Vocational school or trade school students are usually so damaged by the time they reach trade school that they perceive themselves as failures, misfits, and intellectual inferiors. They do not believe that what they are doing has any value, or that they themselves have any personal value, regardless of the psychological systems they may have developed to cover the damage. So, although trade schools may provide a much better opportunity for spiritual growth, they serve only a limited portion of the educational population. And those who do attend have usually had to "fail" to get there.

TEACHING

Teachers claim they are dedicated to real learning. Some believe they are fostering creativity and self-expression. Others say they are preparing children for adult life and teaching people how to operate effectively in the world. None of these claims are true. Teachers are dedicated to upholding the educational system, not to real learning. They are dedicated to lesson plans and school curriculum, not to creativity and self-expression. They do not prepare anyone for adequate functioning in the adult world.

Teachers do not teach children anything about why they are here on the physical plane. They do not tell children about the purpose for incarnation and the need for spiritual growth. They make very few attempts to connect children to the physical world in ways that would promote both mental health and evolution. They know nothing of evolutionary requirements and the need for individual accomplishment and self-expression.

Education is a system of endarkenment designed to punish people for making mistakes and to prevent real learning. Teachers, principals and school officials are the keepers of darkness, who guard their system against any real knowledge or light while claiming to make great educational advances. They promote new ideas, "open classrooms," team teaching, New Age methods. These are all outgrowths of darkness that perpetuate the same incorrect, inadequate system. None of these systems offer real learning. None of these systems were constructed to aid the individual soul. Education and all of its systems are concerned only with the mind.

With very few exceptions, teachers are interested only in the mind. Those few who might wish to offer something of value would be readily snuffed out by the system as it now exists. This is because education is based upon damage in the same way that religion and psychotherapy are based upon damage. Damage begets only more damage.

For the most part, teachers come to education in the same way that clergy come to religion and therapists to the field of mental health. They come with damage and use their positions to protect the damage. Teachers use their minds to protect their damage. More accurately, teachers misuse their minds to protect their damage. They fill their own minds with meaningless, often incorrect information. They remain preoccupied with mental ideas and mind antics that prevent them from looking at the hurt, pain, loneliness and suffering in their lives, all caused by damage. They misuse their students by teaching them to misuse their own minds and to become preoccupied with meaningless mental data.

In many cases, teachers even inflict their damages onto the students. They project their own hurts and pains onto children in the form of contempt, disdain and disapproval. They easily see the vulnerable students. They see the students who are too damaged to protect themselves from teacher projections. They see that they can cause students to feel shameful, unworthy and inadequate by using the power of their position in the classroom.

Teaching offers many the opportunity to continually inflict damage in the name of education. Some resort to physically abusing children in the name of discipline. However, education offers no real discipline. These methods of discipline are simply disguises for damage. Education is full of sophisticated mental reasons for causing damage. Teachers have barricaded themselves against the reality of their own unresolved pain. They have airtight rationalizations for why they disapprove of their students, causing the children to feel so unworthy and inadequate. They have "good" reasons for why they teach what they teach in the way they teach it. However, all their rationalizations and reasons are lies and illusions designed to perpetuate a very dark system.

Educators cover their lies with high tech video equipment, computers and audio-visual aids that appear glamourous, expensive and stimulating. They use anything to keep the system the same while creating the illusion that things are getting better. However, education, like religion, stays exactly the same. There are no schools anywhere on this planet at this time that are dedicated to the evolution of the students' souls. The schools are dedicated only to the misuse of the students' minds. The teachers are dedicated to perpetuating the misuse.

Teachers, like psychotherapists, are proclaimed experts without ever demonstrating any real skill. Even if the same endarkened system remained intact, people might still look at those with whom they are leaving their children. Teachers are automatically hired to teach after four years of education, which is not real learning. They are not asked to demonstrate their ability to operate effectively in the world. They are not asked to maintain any personal standard of mental health. They are not asked to demonstrate any ability to relate effectively to children. They are not asked to demonstrate any ability to deal with the real pain and suffering many children bring to the classroom.

Parents close their eyes. They do not wish to see that they are leaving their children in the hands of people who may not have their children's best interests at heart. They leave their children with teachers who do not know how to teach them or support them. In some cases, parents are leaving their children with child abusers who cause their children to feel worthless, aimless and even hateful toward themselves. However, parents are too asleep and too damaged themselves to stop the system. And teachers are too content misusing their minds to stop abusing their students.

SCIENCE

In order to accomplish spiritual growth, people must first be taught to function in the world. They must receive all the basic, necessary information to allow for a healthy, functioning life. They must receive accurate information about the world and how it operates. Education fails to provide the information necessary for healthy functioning. Even worse, the present system teaches people completely incorrect data about the nature of the universe and the purpose for individual existence.

Education's alleged "science" is a travesty. It is not the study of the world, mankind, or anything it claims to be. If science were a study of the universe, children would be taught the history of this planet. Children would know that the planet earth exists for the purpose of providing a physical world where souls come to grow and learn. They would know that the planet is now emerging from a long period of darkness. Children would be taught about the energetic influences of other planetary bodies upon the earth. They would know that humanity is entering a new era of enlightenment and that the planet Uranus will greatly influence the first two thousand years of this era. They would better understand the chaos and confusion, the turmoil and the instability brought about by the Uranian influence. When they listened to the news or studied current events, they would understand what to expect for this time in their lives and the years ahead. However, science teaches children that the planets are unrelated, disconnected bodies in the sky, limited in number by what can be viewed with the human eye through a telescope.

Children are taught to view the world in a narrow, limited way. They do not learn the extent of the universe because science relies only on the scientific method, completely failing to account for anything that cannot be established through the use of the five senses. So, the extent of this universe and of other worlds remains unconsidered by education.

Since children do not know why they are here, they believe science's idea of the life cycle. They believe that they are born, live an average life span, and then die. Religion provides the afterlife illusions that have nothing to do with the life cycle of the soul. Children are not taught that the life force emanates from the soul. They believe that it comes from the body. They do not learn that souls come from a source known as the spheres of Celestial Origin and that each soul enters incarnation at some level of existence for the purpose of fulfilling that soul's individual destiny. Children are taught that physical death ends the life cycle, so they are afraid to die. They are not taught about the Inner World or that physical death allows the soul to return to the Inner World for rest and further learning before incarnating again.

When children all over the world watched the Challenger Space Shuttle explode they were left in horror, not only from what they had observed, but from the ignorance and misinformation of education and so-called science. If people knew anything about mismatched energy and destiny, the flight would have been cancelled. Children were not told about the energetic causes of this disaster, nor were they told that some of those souls passed into the Inner World. The souls were either guided by the Brotherhood to places of rest and greater learning to prepare for future incarnations, or they went into the lower astral spheres because they refused the Brotherhood's aid. Those souls did not die. The physical vehicles died. Souls exist on a continuum. However, school children everywhere are taught that death is the end. They learn nothing about reincarnation of the soul and the real continuum of life. Children are not told that what they do each day will determine their future lives, so they do not learn to be responsible for their own souls each day. Children are not taught to live responsible, healthy lives which will allow continuous spiritual growth. They are instructed to "take" the most out of life each day because they are going to die anyway. One cannot live a life of selfishness, greed, meaninglessness and disregard and expect to have future lifetimes of growth and evolution.

Science knows nothing of Planetary Hierarchy and the fact that the universe is a physical, somewhat distorted manifestation of Hierarchy. Simply stated, the mineral, vegetable, lower animal, and human kingdoms all represent steps on the ladder of Hierarchy. These kingdoms are not separate, disconnected groups to be memorized by school children for a science test. These kingdoms exist on a continuum. Souls evolve up through this continuum. Children do not learn to respect these kingdoms as the physical reflection of Hierarchy. They learn only unrelated names, classes and scientific categories that keep the reality of Hierarchy disconnected and meaningless.

Science knows nothing of the human consciousness, its psychological or physical functioning. Because science does not acknowledge the reality of reincarnation and the continued life of the individual soul, science fails to account for past life influences and soul memory. Science teaches that the planetary bodies in this universe exist as separate balls in the sky. It therefore fails to acknowledge the energetic influence of each of the planetary bodies on the individual human consciousness. Science knows nothing of astrology and of the fact that people experience a continuous twenty-eight day moon cycle which influences their moods, learning ability, energy levels and much, much more. Science knows nothing about the physical body because it fails to acknowledge that the problems within the body begin in the energetic system surrounding the body. So science is content in developing new drugs and machines to quiet physical symptoms, rather than healing the energetic sources of physical problems.

All science is disconnected, linear misinformation offered by educational systems to perpetuate human ignorance. It gives great acclaim to individual scientists who become glorified for discovering a new piece of disconnected misinformation. So while scientists compete for prizes and government grants, people are led further away from evolution. People are led into irresponsible lives without regard for the soul. They are led away from the real learning and connecting with the world around them required for spiritual growth to take place.

CREATIVITY AND SELF-EXPRESSION

A soul grows when it is able to obtain accurate data in a way that allows it to make connections and to continuously express those connections out into the world. Education not only fails to provide accurate data that would allow souls to make these necessary connections, but also fails to provide any real opportunities for creativity and self-expression. Educators claim to foster creativity, but this is absolutely not true. Education is concerned only with the development of the mind, not the soul, and only offers opportunities for the mind to increase its data bank.

In a real learning situation, a student might study a subject such as geometry. After a few basic classes covering the use of calculating instruments and basic geometric principles, the class would move to the school woodworking shop. There all the geometric principles could be applied to the building of a table or the turning of a bowl on a wood lathe. Students would learn that they must cut two perfect 45 degree angles in order to make the corner of the table. They would see that to draw a circle of wood to make a bowl blank for woodturning, they must know that the radius is half the diameter. If they were unable to make these simple applications, geometry would remain a meaningless, disconnected subject.

After a necessary learning period, students would apply these newly acquired skills to their own individual woodworking projects. Each student would have the opportunity to use his or her own creativity to express these new skills out into the world. Mistakes would not only be allowed, but encouraged and supported. Students would walk away from geometry classes with a genuine understanding of this aspect of the physical universe, and a completed project representing that soul's understanding.

These students would also learn about the motors that run the shop equipment and how motors turn linear motion into rotary motion. They would learn about trees and about one of the important roles trees play in the lives of human beings by providing an essential construction material. They would see which trees make good furniture and how hardwoods are required for bowl turning. They would acquire certain manual skills necessary for healthy ongoing self-expression.

Most important of all, these students would have been given the opportunity to create something and to express some aspect of the consciousness at that time. Education presently does not allow students to receive information in a way that will promote creativity and self-expression. Education gives only linear information that is absorbed into the human memory system or forgotten. It provides few, if any, opportunities for a person to absorb information in a way that will promote creativity and self-expression. As a result, most high school students learn geometry, but cannot remember even basic geometrics by the time they graduate. They cannot remember because they were unable to connect the information to an experience of the real world that would lead to self-expression. In fact, humanity need only look at the lives of high school students to see that education has so dramatically failed.

After the fifth or sixth grade, the human consciousness hungers for individuality and identity, found only in some genuine form of self-expression. Education provides no such avenues, so adolescents, particularly in Western societies, are left to find some way of establishing individuality and identity. These children look to the world of glamour, to rock stars, drugs, clothes, makeup, movie stars, and sex, attempting to find individuality and identity. These children are looking for meaning, for some way to express their own unique consciousness. Education offers rules, memorization, meaninglessness and boredom. Adolescents know their lives are empty. They know they are living without purpose. Humanity accepts the wasted lives of adolescents and blames this mess on the teenagers themselves, rather than on the system that has failed them.

Teenagers approach school as something they have to finish. They think of their classwork as a chore and look forward to getting out. Most do what they can to avoid working too hard while others compete for meaningless academic standing. They all know they are being prepared for meaningless, boring adult lives. No one questions the system, yet very few would say they are experiencing real satisfaction and growth during their adolescent years.

Satisfaction comes through real learning that involves the soul. Satisfaction is only achieved in the spiritual world, not the human world. Soul growth requires continuous learning that sparks creativity and triggers the need for healthy self-expression. Education prevents creativity and curtails self-expression. It has produced a society of glamour-hungry teenagers preparing for meaningless adult lives.

HIGHER EDUCATION

Much emphasis is placed on the value of a college education. Parents and teachers encourage students to seek college degrees, regardless of the students' needs or the immense shortcomings of higher education itself. Societies assume that higher education breeds intelligence and promotes expertise. People believe that a college degree reflects some level of mastery and certifies a professional in his or her field.

Higher education is of no spiritual value at all, and is actually of little human value. Higher education has nothing to do with intelligence or accomplishment. As we have seen in our examination of humanity's psychotherapists, colleges do not create "experts." Higher education is a more sophisticated version of the same darkness that permeates the entire formal education system.

We have already spoken of the lack of real learning experiences offered by formal education; how this system fails to offer souls accurate data and the opportunity to make necessary connections in the real world. We have spoken of the fact that education offers such courses as geometry without connecting geometry to a real life experience such as woodworking. Geometry then becomes a meaningless and disconnected set of information. Higher education offered by colleges and universities creates even less opportunity for real learning and even more serious cases of "disconnectedness." College subjects are generally even less related to the real world, offering students massive amounts of useless mental junk. Souls very rarely grow in college; only minds grow in college. Competitive

people with good memories like college. Souls do not seek to compete or memorize. They seek to learn. College supports education
without errors. Souls learn by making mistakes. Colleges process
students and sometimes offer courses to thousands of students in
huge lecture halls. Souls seek individual destiny, self-expression
and creativity.

Colleges claim to prepare people for their roles in life. Yet, none
of our world leaders were prepared in any way by their college
educations. None were prepared to understand and solve the human problems of poverty, starvation, ignorance, despair or war.
There were no political science courses offered to teach potential
leaders how to reach people and how to help them join together to
solve their problems. Many of our world leaders have studied history, but have learned nothing. College did not teach them to unravel the incorrect ideas and energetic sources of humanity's
problems in the history of the past. Nor does it offer anything to
help humanity in the future.

Higher education does not teach people to become teachers who
offer real learning, or therapists who offer real aid, or ministers who
know anything about real spiritual needs. College does not teach
physicians to use medicine correctly or to seek the energetic causes
for physical problems. It does not teach lawyers to help people
understand laws and standards, or the need for adequate limitations
in a civilized society. College does not offer lawyers the help they
need to simplify the system and to make good laws work for all
people.

Higher education trains people to become more and more disconnected from the real world. It trains physicians and lawyers to
seek high salaries and to become detached from the pain and suffering of their clients. It teaches scientists to work in compart-
mentalized units, competing for government grants while refusing
to share any real discoveries with one another and humanity for
fear of losing funding. Higher education bestows titles and degrees,
but demands no performance in the real world. There are no standards of actual accomplishment, only tests that certify a certain level
of human memory.

Colleges do not teach students about the lights and the electrical
system in the classroom. Most students never learn to change a fuse
or repair simple frayed wires. They know nothing about the cars

they drive to school, or about the metal or wood frame construction of the buildings in which they study. College students do not know where the paper they are writing on comes from or how it is made. Most could not fix the toilet if it broke or repair a leaky faucet. They learn nothing about human relationships, raising children, or balancing a checkbook. In fact, the more educated a person becomes, the less likely he or she is to have or to use any practical skills. More often, the college educated will hire someone to repair their electrical appliances, service their cars and fix their leaky faucets.

As the years pass, the college educated professionals spend more and more time in their minds. Some become like the professors who once taught them—mental nomads who wander aimlessly through life lost in their own minds. College professors are, to a great extent, extremely disconnected from physical world realities. Their lives are nothing but mental illusions, thesis papers and mind chatter. As a group, they are very disturbed, using their minds to the extreme to cover their damages. Their human relationships lack any real compassion or human contact. Their lives reflect much disturbance and pathology, yet they are heralded as the ones who prepare young men and women for their roles in society. They prepare the "experts." In the face of this travesty, it is no wonder that many college students spend their "educational" years drunk, drugged and very lost.

SOUL LEARNING

Souls must be able to learn by making connections in the physical world. In the human sense, this is necessary for normal, healthy functioning in the world. The more a person understands about his or her world, the more that person is able to manage responsibly in the world, to have healthy relationships and a satisfying life.

In the spiritual sense, these connections are of even greater significance. Each consciousness has its own unique wiring system, almost like the electrical wiring in a house. Each soul carries its own unique vibration. Some souls carry a very low vibration while others have a much higher vibration. The vibration of the soul is like the electricity that runs through the wires. Some wiring systems are capable of sustaining only a very low current, while other systems with more adequate wiring can sustain a much stronger current.

The vibration of the individual soul might also be thought of as the amount of light that is on within that soul. Some systems have only enough wires to support a current that will light a very tiny bulb. Other systems are capable of conducting the necessary current to light many rooms, or many areas of the consciousness. Each person generates a certain amount of light. The exceptions are those who have little or no soul connection so that they are literally completely in the dark.

Spiritual growth is a process of slowly connecting the wires in the consciousness so that enough electrical current can flow to sustain higher and higher vibrations and to produce more and more light. The first connections made are between the soul and the human ego structure, then between the soul and the spirit. Spiritual growth cannot take place without this process. There is simply no other way for the human consciousness to lift itself up, or for souls to have any increase in vibration.

These connections are unique for each person and are accomplished in ways that are available and acceptable to an individual consciousness. An added requirement is that each person must be able to correct specific wires at specific times. If people imagined themselves wiring a house, for instance, they would see that the wires must be placed according to instructions and in a specific order. One cannot expect the second floor of a house to provide light when the wiring to the main circuits has not yet been completed in the basement. So too with souls. A person must connect the wires in his or her consciousness in a somewhat orderly and timely way. We say somewhat because the system is far from perfect and connections are sometimes made that are not necessarily sequential. In the spiritual sense, however, souls cannot move from the vibration of a first degree initiate to the vibration of a fourth degree initiate without completing the second and third initiations. The consciousness would not have ample wiring to support the vibration of the fourth level without completing each of the preceding steps. The consciousness could not conduct the electrical force to sustain the light of the fourth without having laid all the proper wiring for the first through the third.

The wires exist energetically in the consciousness and the connections must therefore be accomplished energetically. However, these wires and connections do have representations in the physical world. So when a person is able to connect the fact that the angles studied in geometry class can be applied to the construction of a table (which was once a tree), certain energetic wires in the consciousness, represented by the meeting of angles to make the corners and legs of the table, can be energetically connected. Not every soul would necessarily benefit from these particular external events, but many souls would be able to make some connections through such experiences. Learning geometry as a separate subject, without any physical world application, will cause "disconnectedness." This learning experience is directly opposite from the experience necessary to provide spiritual growth.

If people were able to continuously make connections, ongoing evolution could once again become possible. The physical world exists in order to provide people with external physical representations of their own internal wiring. By properly manipulating and connecting these external representations, internal energetic connections can be accomplished. When humanity fails to see the purpose of the physical universe, and fails to properly utilize the external representations of their own inner wiring, evolution remains impossible. Souls cannot grow without making the connections that will allow the electrical current to flow and the vibration to increase. Without this current, the individual consciousness has little or no light and literally remains in the dark.

5

SOCIAL BARRIERS TO EVOLUTION

POVERTY

People like to think that poverty is a small problem involving a small portion of the world population. This idea enables most of humanity to remain safely blinded to the plight of many souls in need of help. Poverty affects two-thirds of this planet. Millions of souls are caught in cycles of starvation, disease, homelessness and despair. These souls have no energy or resources to break from these cycles because all of their energies are used each day just to survive.

These souls are, for the most part, bankrupt. They cannot grow nor do they even aspire to grow. They seek only enough food to survive the day and enough shelter to provide protection from rain and cold. They do not expect normal lifespans. They expect to die from the disease and malnutrition that they call life. These souls do not seek fulfilling relationships nor do they expect their children to have better lives. They expect hunger, poverty and homelessness. They expect despair. They are so severely damaged and so beaten down that they are very often reattracted to the same circumstances lifetime after lifetime.

Humanity does not want to see the extent of the problem or the fact that the solutions do not lie in the hands of the poor. Most of humanity actually expect these souls to somehow uplift themselves. People do not want to see the spiritual bankruptcy that poverty and starvation create. They want to believe that the poor could work harder and somehow fight their own way out of despair.

Humanity does not want to see the effect of poverty on the planet at large. People refuse to look at the fact that the lives and the well-being of others influence the kind of world in which they all live. It is as though people believe the earth is carved up into small separate planets—some for the rich, some for the poor, and some for those in between. They want to think that these smaller units are not energetically connected to the larger system, or that no one has any responsibility outside of his own self-contained unit. This mentality allows governments such as the United States to pay farmers not to grow food and to slaughter "unneeded" dairy cows, while two-thirds of the world suffers from hunger and malnutrition. This kind of thinking causes governments to spend millions of dollars on "military aid" to less fortunate countries, while offering much less and sometimes nothing to feed and clothe the people of those countries. It allows governments to buy guns, bombs, and military uniforms rather than medicines, vaccines and sanitation systems. People refuse to see that humanity is a unit and that the earth is their home. They choose not to understand that no matter where they live, poverty and disease exist in their own back yard.

There are more than enough resources on this planet to solve the problems of poverty. There is plenty of food and available water. There are large amounts of building materials for shelter and an abundance of land for good homes. There are plenty of warm clothes for everyone and an overabundance of money and people power to accomplish the task. There is simply a world-wide lack of interest.

Some would say there is not a lack of interest and that people are helping the poor now. They would say there are many projects, concerts, and fundraising activities to provide for these souls. For the most part this is, unfortunately, not true. Most of these programs and projects have actually caused the poor more difficulties than ever before.

These programs and concerts offered to raise money for the poor may actually have started out with good intentions. Some people may truly have believed that by offering their ability and talent to make a record album or act in a television show, they were offering something that would raise funds to be used by the poor. They could not see that glamour is itself a problem for humanity. One cannot use a problem to solve a problem. So, those who sang for the hungry are now more famous because they sang for the hungry. They are nominated for more awards and will receive more record contracts in the future. Their personal lives have only been improved because they sang for the hungry. Because of glamour, the energy that should have gone into solving the problems of the poor has been robbed, in some cases very unintentionally, but nonetheless robbed. The energy that would have been used to cause others to respond to the needs of the poor has gone into the careers of the musicians. They have essentially used the hungry to become more well-known, more famous, more wealthy. They are musical heroes at the expense of the poor.

Those who offered their talents for the homeless created more homelessness. They called attention to the problem through glamour and therefore glamourized the problem. They actually caused people to see homelessness as a glamourous condition. They did not address the real problem underlying homelessness, which is personal failure. Homeless people have acquired an idea of themselves, through education, that they are personal failures. They are often simply caught in the idea. Many of these people have the ability and skills to earn a living and to find themselves an adequate home, but are caught in the idea of personal failure. Homelessness is now on the increase because it is now a more glamourous condition than ever before. Even those who are genuinely bankrupt and unable to combat poverty and homelessness have been robbed of any energy they might have accumulated before the problem became glamourous.

Those who sincerely work to provide aid to the poor are not famous, nor do they live glamourous lives that could potentially rob those in need of aid. They are the quiet ones who work behind the scenes under nearly impossible circumstances, without adequate support. However, they are too few and their access to real resources is too limited to have any noticeable effect on the problems of the poor and hungry.

POWER VS. LEADERSHIP

Humanity suffers from an extreme lack of real leadership. Very few countries are led by people who are genuinely concerned about those they claim to lead. All of the major world leaders are concerned only with protecting their own damages through the misuse of human will and the accumulation of personal power. None of these leaders seek peace nor do they act on behalf of their people, no matter what they claim to be doing.

Just as humanity views the poor as separate from the rich, so do people view countries as separate, independent entities. They vehemently protect their borders and will even fight wars to protect this idea of separateness. People fail to see any energetic relationship between and among the countries of the world. They see products that can be imported or exported for convenience or financial gain, but fail to see any of the necessary energetic connections and relationships. People do not feel responsible for the people of other countries, so they see no need to share resources in ways that would support worldwide well-being. In fact, countries abundant in certain resources see the opportunity to exploit other countries lacking in that particular resource. They see an opportunity to raise the price of oil, wheat, sugar, or other essential commodities, and to gain financially from another country's weakness. The more essential the resource, the greater the potential for exploitation to occur.

People see those from other countries as "foreigners," "aliens," and even enemies. They are usually frightened of one another and approach each other from self-protection rather than with any real welcome or desire to share. Countries protect their resources as they protect their boundaries, causing scarcity and fear rather than abundance and sharing.

World leaders prey upon these fears caused by separations. They use humanity's misguided ideas to amass much personal power. Many world leaders are what the Brotherhood calls "original faulters," and what humanity might call original sinners. Original fault exists in the consciousness of about 58 percent of the world population. Original fault might better be termed original heartbreak. These souls, somewhere along the line, all incurred some devastating experience that damaged the individual consciousness beyond repair. Because the damage was so severe, original faulters used their free will to protect the damaged areas, often constructing elaborate behavior patterns that prevented them from ever again experiencing the pain of that original damage. Original faulters come from lifetimes of misused free will and self-protection, including lifetimes of inflicting pain on others in order to avoid feeling pain themselves. They have only their self-protected interests at heart.

Over 90 percent of today's world leaders suffer from original fault and have developed many intricate, manipulative behavior patterns that are now used to amass and hold power over the lives of others. They see the weaknesses and fears in their people. They use these fears to build elaborate weapon systems and to keep people from sharing their resources and solving their problems. They allot funds only to projects that will bring them votes. When people have a problem such as water pollution or lead poisoning, they must first bring that problem to the media for public attention. They must interest enough voters to make their problems worth solving. Those who suffer but are not able to accumulate voter attention are simply left to suffer. In this way, world leaders appear to be responding to the needs of their people while they are simply gaining more power, more approval and more self-importance.

World leaders have absolutely no concern for peace. They are concerned only with self-protection, to the point of war if necessary. They want only to protect their own ideas of power. They talk of peace while they are designing new weapons for war.

World leaders keep souls living in scarcity and in fear. They have no desire to solve problems through cooperation and sharing. They have no desire to free souls from the damages and chronic behavior patterns perpetuated by fear. If they are leading anything, they are leading souls further away from spiritual growth and further into darkness and separateness.

Souls can only grow in peace and quiet. They cannot grow in a world of violence, chaos and fear. Souls simply cannot be heard when terrorism and chaos rule people's lives. These world leaders will soon be losing ground. People will come to see the Reagans, Marcos, and Gadhafis for what they really are. Unfortunately, there will be much upheaval before real world leaders can come to office. Many will suffer during the transition, as those hungry only for personal power fade away. The Age of Enlightenment promises humanity real leadership, but not without many battles with those who seek only personal gain.

GLAMOUR

Humanity has become dangerously preoccupied with glamour, comfort and convenience. People are literally bombarded every day with sensational vacation offers, flashy cars, bizarre hairstyles, exotic and often uncomfortable clothes, the need for thin, perfect bodies and the importance of using makeup. People look to movie stars and famous athletes as their role models. They want high tech lives and stereophonic comfort. They aspire toward executive positions, large salaries, fame, and fortune with no interest, regard or concern for the fact that people are souls with purposes to fulfill.

Glamour now consumes much of the human energy needed for evolution. Glamour devalues anything spiritual and values only the "hype" and the "excitement" of the moment. Glamour causes many problems to humanity that will be very difficult to unravel because glamour is so appealing to the human ego.

Glamour robs souls of much-needed energy, and ties that energy up in the human personality, causing people to misspend their resources. People do not understand that they have a limited amount of energetic resources. If those resources are correctly used, souls are able to regenerate themselves and actually create more energy. Only souls can regenerate. Human ego structures cannot generate life force. So, when the human personality consumes the resources in the consciousness on something like glamour, the person is simply left spent, without any energy to cause growth and regeneration of the soul. Once a person is spent, it is very difficult to regenerate. It can be done in the physical world, but only under very specific conditions and with a kind of personal commitment and focus not found in those who spend their resources on glamour. These souls must usually wait until physical death when they can pass into the Inner World and get the rest and regeneration necessary, assuming they follow the instructions given to them at physical death.

When souls are fulfilling their own destiny and purpose, they have no time or interest in glamour. If people looked at the life of Mother Teresa, they would not find a woman concerned with her hair color and makeup. She does not get up every day and put on a satin running outfit to jog three miles with her headphones. She does not plan exotic vacations for herself or try to emulate television characters and movie stars. She is a soul with a specific purpose, dedicated to fulfilling that purpose, and cannot afford to spend herself on anything else. Not every soul was destined to feed the hungry of India, but each soul on this planet has an equally important purpose and reason for being here.

Glamour is today a much more serious problem than ever before. Even fifty or a hundred years ago, people were not barraged as they are today. Their lives were much simpler. They were concerned about basics, not sensationalism and excitement in the way that many people are today. Many human egos use glamour to protect their damages, while others are simply hooked on the excitement.

Those who use glamour to protect their hurts do not want to look at the pain and sorrow underneath the makeup and flashy clothes. They do not want to see the emptiness behind the seemingly "right" relationship. They are the women who use thick makeup on their faces to cover their degrading feelings about their own sexual nature. They are the ones who were abused by men in the past or present, or taught by religion that their bodies were dirty and evil. The more makeup they use, the deeper their personal condemnation and pain.

They are the men who are caught trying to prove they are men, who refuse to see their weaknesses or feel their hurt and pain. They want only to drive the right car, have the right woman beside them, wear the right clothes, and do the right job. They have completely lost touch with their personal needs or with any notion of what makes them happy. They are too busy covering their inner hurts with ideas of manhood to know anything about themselves.

Then, there are those who are hooked on the "hype" and the "excitement" of glamour. They like being "psyched." They like getting high and are bored by the peace required for evolution. Even when their damages are energetically removed, they still remain trapped in glamour. They misuse their wills to stay in painful and even dangerous relationships that they find exciting. They use their wills to find more of the same danger and excitement long after the damage that once propelled them into such situations has been removed. Spiritual growth cannot occur in a consciousness that is hyped and psyched. Souls need peace and calm, not speed, loud music and bright colors.

Glamour calls to humanity like the Sirens to Ulysses. It promises good times, great taste, and big rewards. However, if people would look closely, they could see that behind the bright lights and good times, there is nothing but an empty void. They would see the great dissatisfaction in the lives of Hollywood's stars, and the continuous need to fill the emptiness with more of the same dissatisfaction. Sadly, many teenagers and young children have begun to emulate these empty lives and aspire for the same dissatisfaction and emptiness. They have already begun to spend their resources on makeup, clothes, music and excitement. They have already accepted glamour over spiritual growth and confusion over peace. They are well on the way to robbing their souls through misuse of the will, thereby decreasing the possibility of any future growth.

ECONOMIC SYSTEMS

The economic systems of the world are largely built upon selfishness, greed, and possessiveness, which cover the damages of those who perpetuate these systems. These systems are not designed to provide a stable standard of living for the masses. They are not based on the sharing of resources and cooperative living. These systems function to provide continued wealth to the few at the expense of the many.

Souls can grow in environments where human needs are met and a suitable, healthy standard of living is maintained. As we have stated, souls cannot grow in lives of starvation and poverty, where all of their resources are spent surviving each day. Nor do souls need lives of personal wealth, where all the energy is spent protecting financial accumulations. Souls can thrive in environments that provide basic material well-being.

The world's economic system is not dedicated to maintaining a healthy standard of living for every soul on the planet. It is a system of the "haves" and the "have nots." It is a system designed to insure the economic security of the "haves," even if it is at the expense of the "have nots." It is a system where neighbors do not support neighbors; where an individual gains even at a neighbor's expense. This system allows some farmers to suffer severe financial losses, while their more fortunate neighbors buy up their farm equipment at auction. It is a system where people think nothing of selling products to other people who do not need them or cannot afford them. It is a ruthless system because no one wants to see that one man's personal gain is often another man's personal loss.

Selfishness and greed emanate from the human ego. Therefore, they are desires without limits and simply cannot be permanently satisfied no matter how much wealth is gained. So many of the rich say they will be satisfied when they earn, for example, a quarter of a million dollars. Yet few, if any, can stop there. Most automatically increase their hypothetical satisfaction point to a half or even a full million and so on. The selfish and the greedy are truly the proverbial donkeys chasing one economic carrot after another. They think they will be satisfied with one new car, but then find out they want another. They think a ten room house will be enough, but then find out they want twenty rooms. They think ten pairs of shoes will cover all their fashion concerns, but then discover another dozen colors that they just must have. While millions of feet ache every night because they go without the protection of shoes all day, wealthy men and women are every day building larger closets to accommodate their expanding wardrobes without any regard for the rest of humanity's aches.

Almost all economic systems, even those that claim to support the masses, are built on selfishness and greed, and designed to support the few at the expense of the many. There are few laws that require the wealthy to aid the less fortunate. There are no standards to regulate how much can be acquired and at whose expense. There is very little sharing even among those who claim to be family and friends. People who give their money away to others are often thought foolish. Most people think instead that if they earn "it" or acquire "it," there is no financial responsibility to anyone or anything else.

Because economic systems are based on selfishness and greed, which have no boundaries, countries have no boundaries in their spending. Today's economy is completely artificial. It is constructed out of manufactured paper without any backing for the dollar. Governments and individual people generally operate in the red. They have lost sight of the need for balance and economic stability. They are too busy spending their paper to see that such a system is destined to fail through collapse.

Governments do not understand the price of inflation or the energetic principle that what goes up, must come down. They do not see that balance is necessary in every way to maintain a stable economic system, and that each imbalanced condition will require an equal, opposite imbalance before balance can once again be achieved.

People are trained to overspend. They are encouraged throughout the world's system to use charge cards now and pay later without regard for the fact that they are overspending. People have no boundaries on what they spend and believe there are no repercussions for their spending.

The economic systems of the world are completely dark systems maintained by people whose lives are run by personal selfishness and greed. These systems are still on the rise, but are due to collapse and fall so that balance can be restored. Those who misuse their economic resources, and have the most invested in maintaining the economic system as it now exists, will suffer the most. Those who work every day to preserve their investments and to earn their desired paychecks will face much pain and emptiness. They will be jolted at the collapse of some insurance companies, banking systems and stock certificates, because they have placed all their energy into these systems and no energy into their souls. Those who live moderate lives will suffer least. However, all will feel the collapse of this economic darkness because the system is at this time simply destroying itself.

ENVIRONMENTAL DESTRUCTION

Due to not understanding the ongoing life of the soul and the facts of reincarnation, most people believe they live a single lifetime and die at physical death. They do not believe they are responsible for what they do with a given lifetime. They see no connection between what they do now and what results and problems they might incur later. Further, people have no understanding of the purpose and proper use of the physical world. Therefore, they have no respect for the physical world and see no need to properly tend to their own evolutionary classrooms. Many on this planet literally treat the world as a gigantic waste site. They poison their own water and food supplies. They pollute and destroy the air needed to breathe. They needlessly kill precious animal life for personal pleasure and toy with chemical wastes they know nothing about.

Humanity allows people to experiment with nuclear power and

to build nuclear devices that even "scientists" know nothing about. Nuclear engineers know nothing of subatomic structures. They cannot clairvoyantly see what they are playing with nor do they have any idea about safely handling it. Scientists are well aware that nuclear radiation has some effect on people, but they have no idea how to control this effect. Nuclear energy is subatomic. It cannot be seen or observed with any of the five senses. It actually affects some people positively, meaning that some people feel they are thriving next to their local nuclear plant. It affects some people very negatively by activating weak areas in the consciousness and inciting serious diseases such as cancer. Those who want nuclear power do not care about these negative and painful effects on their fellow human beings. They do not care that scientists do not yet know how to adequately regenerate nuclear wastes. They do not care about the potential long-term dangers in storing products that are beyond their understanding. They care only about that which can be gained right now without any regard for present or future planetary effects. They cannot see the mess they are making and the potential effects of this mess on the human race for thousands of years to come. They do not see that the people who are making these problems now are the same people who will have to find solutions in the generations ahead.

This same mentality exists in those who manufacture products that cause polluting residues found in air, water and food. Most of these manufacturers know that their company produces hazardous waste products. They know they must dispose of these waste products. They know they are dumping them into the world land and water supply. They care only about the profits to be made. They know they would not allow these products to be dumped behind their own homes where their own lives might be endangered. People will not hear stories of company presidents who dump hazardous wastes into their upper class neighborhoods. They will more readily hear of companies closing and of presidents leaving the area when called upon to clean up the mess they were responsible for making. This occurs because people have no idea of the spiritual debts they incur through such irresponsible action. They completely misunderstand the laws of karma that automatically hold us responsible for everything we do here. They do not understand that as souls they must balance their scales. If they have lived their lives persecuting others, then they will automatically spend equal time as victims in future lives.

The laws of karma do not exist to provide punishment that equals the crime. Karma is more like the law of energetic balance in the world. It is sacred spiritual law that holds people responsible for their actions. Karma is simply cause and effect. If a person causes something to occur, he or she must experience the effects of that event whether those effects are positive or negative. People completely fail to see that using the world as a toxic waste site will affect the life of the soul no matter how things may appear right now.

People not only believe they can pollute and destroy things in the physical world without responsibility for their acts, they also believe they can pollute and poison people in their lives. People believe they can spend fifty years in hurtful marriage relationships, destroying and damaging one another every day without incurring any karmic debt. They believe they can emotionally or even physically abuse their children in the name of proper parenting or that they can underpay their employees in the name of good capitalism without any repercussions. These are not disguised threats of hell and damnation. Karmic law has nothing to do with hell, purgatory or heaven. It has to do with cause and effect, and with balancing the scales.

If people truly understood the spiritual laws that govern this planet, they would not inflict destruction and pollution on the physical world or on one another. If people knew the precious and necessary role the physical world has in the evolution of humanity, they would not try to destroy it. If people knew the potential problems that lie ahead for themselves as souls, that are being set in motion now, they would not act so ruthlessly toward their environments and toward one another.

MEDICINE

Societies throughout the world look to the medical profession for both physical and emotional healing. They look to physicians as healers and seek their help at very vulnerable times. However, medicine is no longer a healing profession. It is a lucrative career. Most men and women who now study to become doctors, do not do so to serve humanity. If they were truly interested in serving humanity they would not survive medical school. They instead seek careers where large salaries can be made from the pain of sick people.

Medicine is now a world of high finance. Physicians are much more interested in hearing from their stockbrokers than in hearing from a patient in pain. They offer one standard of care to the rich or well-insured and another to the poor and elderly. They see no obligation to humanity at large, no need to give anything of themselves without a guaranteed fee for "service."

Because physicians are far more attracted to the dollar than to the well-being of people, they misuse their positions and exploit the helplessness and vulnerability of their patients. They do nothing to address the emotional pains and fears of the sick. They offer very little compassion or support. In fact, far more often they offer rudeness, criticism and disdain. They treat people as though the people were annoying them, while charging high fees to administer this mistreatment. People are afraid to call doctors when they are sick. They are afraid of the mistreatment and abuse.

Physicians offer mistreatment as a way of passing off their own unresolved damages to their patients. Teachers use students. Clergy use church members. Physicians use sick people. They know the power and authority that medicine and society offer them. They know people need advice and medicines. They are very damaged with many personal problems. Many of them have personal lives that are ridden with alcoholism, drug abuse, unsuccessful relationships, and much unresolved pain. However, like most in humanity, they cover their damages with chronic behavior patterns—with glamour, power and money. They treat their patients with contempt, disdain and disapproval as a way of continuously passing off their own damage to others. Many literally dump their own hurts and damages into their patients, causing some people to get worse when they should be getting better.

This emotional dumping can be accomplished through critical words and negative attitudes, and it can also be done energetically during surgical procedures and medical treatments. Many people would be appalled to see the damage inflicted upon them during surgery. They would be horrified to see the structural damage to the aura, and the energetic poisons and toxins inflicted into the consciousness of one who is literally "under the knife." This emotional dumping is easily accomplished because people are often too sick and weak to ward off mistreatment and abuse. They are helpless and vulnerable and just cannot resist. Some patients intuitively know they are frightened of more than just the physical procedures. They can feel themselves tighten up into emotional knots when conversing with their physicians. Some patients know that something very wrong is happening. However, the medical profession covers its darknesses, and then maintains a secret agreement not to uncover or reveal one another's abuses, no matter how dangerous or destructive individual behaviors might be. The doctors have the power, granted by the patients and maintained by the system. They have beautiful homes, fancy cars and enjoy exotic vacations, all of which they feel they have earned because they were able to survive medical school. It is a dark, tight system with very few cracks of light.

Because medicine is a system of darkness, it has no understanding or regard for souls. Physicians, and most other people, operate on the idea that the body is the source of life. They do not see that the soul gives life to the body, so that the body can be used by the soul to accomplish spiritual growth. They develop elaborate procedures to keep bodies alive while souls are often attempting to leave the pain of the body through physical death and return to the Inner World for regeneration and repair.

Physicians know nothing about the human consciousness. They think medical problems exist inside the physical body, so they treat only the physical symptoms. They cannot yet see that the sources of most physical problems actually begin in the aura or energy surrounding the physical body. They do not see that physical problems actually begin as nonphysical, energetic breaks and damages to the consciousness. They know many physical symptoms are chronic and that treatment in many cases offers only temporary relief. However, they know nothing of the energetic structure and function of the human consciousness, so they continually look in the wrong places for answers. For all the billions of dollars spent on cancer research, this disease still rages out of control. Medical researchers are simply looking in the wrong places for their answers.

Because physicians know so little about the consciousness, they develop appalling procedures such as heart transplants. They do not understand anything about the spiritual function of a literal "broken heart." They know nothing of the overall damage done to a consciousness by this surgical procedure and the future problems that will have to be unraveled by the soul of the recipient. They do not understand how desperate these souls are to return to the Inner World, and why so few transplants have any long-term success. Physicians are too caught in the fame and glory offered to them as they seem to be so dramatically "saving lives."

Physicians have little regard for the actual effects of drugs and many medical procedures on the consciousness. Many are paid to "experiment" with certain drugs. Others receive college scholarships and grants from drug companies that later expect some return for their "generosity." Most physicians have no idea of the damage done to people by certain drugs and treatments. When they are aware, they consider this damage a so-called "side effect." If they could see the effects of radiation treatments and the devastation done to the consciousness through radiation therapy, they would be horrified beyond words. If they could see these patients through the eyes of the Inner World, they would see burned, charred and mutilated auras that will require much repair before the soul can ever again grow. Medicine is not for souls. There are a few correct, inspired treatments. The discovery of penicillin, for instance, has been of great value to humanity, although the current abuse of antibiotics is not. Medicine is not for service nor is it for healing. Anyone entering this field truly wanting to help would find little support, much disappointment, and probably could not last very long.

SERVICE

To serve others is to give of oneself for no personal gain or reward, except perhaps for the satisfying feeling one might have for having given. Service is a kind of help or aid to others that is nothing else but help and aid. Serving has nothing to do with doing "good" deeds or kind acts, or being a "good" person. It offers no rewards, financial remuneration, fame, prestige, or glory. The energy of service is the only remedy for the problems of darkness and barriers to evolution that humanity now faces.

The energy of pure service is necessary to combat darkness because it is the only energy that can generate enough continued light and fire. When people offer their time or energy to solve a problem, that time and energy can only have a positive effect on the problem if the people are doing genuine acts of service. However, if, for example, the people are doing a good deed by using their musical ability to sponsor a program for the hungry, then they inadvertently or unintentionally draw the original energy intended for the hungry back to themselves. So, while they call great attention to the problem, they actually pull that attention back to their own careers—to greater fame and future wealth. The original energy may have been well-intended and initially directed at the problems of poverty. However, it becomes unavoidably diverted away from hunger and back into the darkness inherent in the gain of personal fame and wealth. In this example, energy that began as light was misdirected from the problem back into darkness. Sadly, the overall, long-term effect on the problem of poverty is to increase it, initially energizing the problem and then withdrawing the energy needed for continued effort at solving the problem. The problem gets lost in the fame and the glamour, and it actually becomes more difficult to bring ongoing relief to the poor.

This is true with any good deed that stands to bring gain to the one offering help. If people look closely, they will see new recording stars as a result of "Live Aid." Many more entertainers will continue this trend because they see what these musicians have gained. If movie stars gain personal fame or success through their "good" deeds, they do nothing but glamourize the problems of humanity. Homelessness is now a very glamourous condition, destined to attract more teenagers and young adults than ever before.

Many would claim to be offering service. However, very few are actually interested in the long-term sacrifices necessary to uplift humanity. It is said by the Brotherhood that many are called, but few choose. There are people who fool themselves and others into thinking that some service is being offered. Some psychotherapists actually believe they are serving. They pretend they are helping people while charging them, or the insurance companies, for the opportunity to project their own unresolved pain. This is definitely not service. Many physicians think they are serving others while they mistreat their patients emotionally and physically in the name of service. They tend carefully to their stock accounts and watch the poor of the world die needlessly from very treatable physical problems. They are not serving. Many politicians claim to serve, yet they act only to support their own political careers. Very few would help with an "unpopular" problem or one that would not bring future votes.

Then, there is the romanticized notion of the teacher serving the children in the classroom. Some children would be less damaged by spending their days with convicted child molesters, because they would at least know what they were up against. Even well-meaning educators only perpetuate disconnected information that prevents soul evolution and eventually curtails learning ability. They are not serving.

Most people cannot yet truly serve because they carry too much damage and hurt. They are too preoccupied with covering and protecting that damage through the misuse of will. They cannot yet see the need to sacrifice their personal pain and suffering because they have spent so long protecting it. They are too conditioned to feeding the human ego demands to see that the human ego is insatiable. They cannot see that the ego will readily rob any available energy to perpetuate its own cause, even if that energy was intended to solve the problems of the poor or homeless, or any in humanity that need uplifting.

Our economic problems cannot be solved by our economic leaders nor our educational darknesses by school administrators. Great and quiet acts of service are needed everywhere. Ironically, service is the only efficient path of evolution now available. Souls cannot get past the third initiation to the fourth without the beginnings of service. That is not to say that all fourth degree initiates are now serving, because they are not. However, souls must reach enough personal detachment and unselfishness to ever return to their original spirit homes.

To do genuine service, one must continuously sacrifice one's personal hurts and wounds. People doing service cannot use their energies to protect damage, so they must release themselves from it. To protect damage is to rob the energy of service for personal gain and reward. Very few would be willing to sacrifice their damages, even when offered the simple technology of the Brotherhood that will easily alleviate the energetic sources of pain.

Many believe that by donating to their favorite "cause" or charity, they are serving. It is true that financial support will be necessary to solve humanity's problems. However, most donations are given for some self-serving purpose, and are often given to "causes" and programs that actually work against the growth of souls. Many people think that if they can write a check for charity, this will justify their overall lack of concern for the well-being of their own families, neighbors and fellow human beings. Some think they can buy their way into heaven by supporting their churches on Sunday, while abusing their spouses and children the rest of the time. Because people are trying to buy some illusion of their own "goodness," they act out of darkness and end up giving the most financial support to those "causes" that provide no real aid. People support things that do not work and mediocrity that offers no help because they act from selfishness, not service.

The Age of Aquarius is a time of cooperation, sharing and service. Humanity will learn much about service in the years ahead, since true service will be required if current human problems are to be solved. There are a few souls who now serve, but they do not seek fame, fortune or success. They only seek more opportunities to serve. They act quietly without the noise and glamour of the human ego, and they only look to do what must be done every day. Unfortunately, they are so few and the problems are many.

6

THE JOURNEY

THE EVOLUTIONARY JOURNEY begins with the origin of each soul. All souls connected to the planet earth originated from one of six spheres known as the planes of Celestial Origin. These planes house the spirit, the personal God of each soul, called the Monad. On the celestial planes, souls establish their original purpose for existence. They then enter into the earthly kingdoms to begin fulfilling that purpose.

Souls exist only to fulfill their own purpose or destiny. They undertake the journey into the evolutionary planes so that this purpose can be fulfilled. Under the best of circumstances, souls remain connected to their own spiritual source or Monad and receive continued direction and guidance from the spirit. Unfortunately, the Age of Darkness has left humanity in the worst possible circumstances, disconnected from their own source or origin.

Although very few souls enjoy the guidance of their own spirit, the spirit of each soul rests in waiting. Spirits exist in deep meditation waiting for souls to accomplish enough evolutionary growth to make reconnection possible. Again, the only way a soul can return to its true spiritual home is through evolution, ongoing learning and growth.

In the wake of so many years of darkness, learning and growing for any soul are nearly impossible. Evolution is an extremely difficult upward climb. There is only one road of evolution regardless of recent claims about "many" paths. The Brotherhood tells us to think of this single road as a stairway that must be climbed. However, this stairway is more like an escalator, and the escalator is slowly and constantly moving down. The Age of Darkness has claimed the "up" escalator. The only way, then, for a soul to return to its spiritual home is to climb *up* the "down" escalator.

It is very difficult to climb up a "down" escalator. The Brotherhood suggests that readers attempt this experience so they can begin to understand what the journey of evolution is actually like. It should also be remembered that this escalator is crowded with people moving down as a few souls attempt to climb up, against the traffic. The faster a person tries to climb upward, the angrier the people become who are going down. This anger makes the climb more difficult for the souls attempting to go up.

Once a person begins the climb, he or she cannot afford to stop. The escalator is always moving downward. If a person tries to stop growing and take a rest, he or she will simply be carried back down the escalator. Souls, then, cannot stop growing and stay still. They will always be carried back down.

It takes no effort to travel down the "down" escalator. People who are moving downward are not required to make personal sacrifices of any kind. They can fill their lives with comfort, convenience, and ideas of personal happiness. They can search for the perfect relationship and marry the person of their dreams. They can program their children into all of their own idealized thoughtforms, earn large salaries and maintain as much power as they want over other people. The downward track is relatively easy and people can take all their baggage with them.

The climb upward against the traffic is very difficult, much too difficult for anyone to attempt carrying heavy baggage. The climb requires great personal sacrifice and extreme inconvenience, which is why so few souls will even consider the climb.

Each soul has a limited amount of time to climb, usually lasting only a few lifetimes. During this time, the soul will find the opportunities and resources necessary to make the climb possible. If a person starts the climb, but then decides to stop, he or she might drift down even farther than the soul's original starting point. The soul must then simply wait for a time when the opportunity and resources are once again available. If a person drops back after having climbed some distance, he or she will find much personal pain and loss because that soul will have known the benefits and the peace of a higher consciousness. They will find both the pain of waiting and the loss of peace difficult to bear.

People are warned, then, not to start unless they plan to finish. They should not climb the escalator unless they want to evolve as much as they want to breathe. Once they find the light, it is very painful to return to darkness, and it is extremely difficult to once again find any light.

Most of humanity will not even begin the climb. They will cling to their ideas that religion is "spiritual," or that psychotherapy is healing, or that education provides learning. They will cling to their comforts, their "ideal" relationships, and their illusions of growing. They will insist that the darkness is light and that the "down" escalator is taking them upward to heaven.

No matter what a person thinks or believes, everyone in humanity is on the escalator. People are either being carried down into darkness away from their spiritual homes or they are battling their way upward against all odds. In this sense, there is only one path of evolution and everyone is on it. Each soul must decide which way to go. The Brotherhood is here to help humanity make the climb. However, even with this help, very few will start the climb and even fewer will keep moving. There will be many years before humanity can see the need to climb and the importance of returning home. For the few who might try, there will be many obstacles, many sacrifices, and very little support from the physical world.

DAMAGE

According to the Brotherhood, if humanity could see themselves from the Inner World's point of view, and could observe the human consciousness through etheric vision, they would see much hurt and pain. People would see a vast number of weary, war-torn souls who are too wounded to attempt any evolutionary climb. They would see auras that appear broken and fragmented, and people covered with gray and black collections of long-term suffering.

Throughout this book we have spoken of the profound effects of unhealed damage on all of humanity. We have spoken of the chronic behavior patterns that people develop to protect their hurts and wounds. These damages and accompanying behavior patterns not only cause humanity great pain, but prevent evolution from taking place. Souls are too worn out and damaged to climb. They have no resources or energy to do anything except protect their damages. Most people now spend a great portion of their life energies just trying to avoid hurt. They have nothing left over to use for spiritual growth.

Damage occurs when people are deeply hurt, physically wounded, or suffer great personal loss. Over the last 75,000 years, the earth has been a dark, violent, and often uncivilized place to live, where souls have been easily damaged. There has been almost no proper healing of these damages, so souls have had to carry the damages from one lifetime to another. Hurts are carried energetically and actually appear as breaks and holes in the aura. The aura was intended to provide a protective shield around the person to ward off some physical diseases and hurtful emotional exchanges.

Damaged areas act like magnetic fields. They not only fail to provide the intended protection, but also pull toward themselves energy like the damage itself. At this time, people are much more attracted to one another by damage than by anything else. They come together and, for the most part, simply perpetuate their hurts. Men and women form marriages out of damage. Parents and children are attracted to one another out of damage. People cannot grow because they cannot stop repeating the same life circumstances. They keep changing the characters with the hope of finding something better.

When men and women come together out of damage to form a relationship, they are unable to use that relationship for spiritual growth or support. This is the most common form of marriage. Women who have past and present life histories involving abusive men, marry abusive men. Women who have histories involving alcoholic, insane, unstable men, seek the excitement and damage of alcoholic, unstable and insane husbands. Women who grow up with fathers who do not like them, marry men who do not like them.

Men who have past or present life histories of overpowering, domineering women, seek the same in their marriage partners. Men who live with crazy mothers look for crazy women to marry. The consciousness simply falls in love with whatever it knows, and seeks to repeat its own history by continually attracting others with similar damage.

So-called "gay" men and women have completely lost their ability to relate. Most are actually here to regain these abilities. However, the damage causes them to attract others who cannot relate. They form empty, unfulfilling relationships that rarely last, because neither person knows anything about relating. They use sex in exploitative, violent ways and completely misuse their sexual energies. They know nothing about the balancing of polarities inside themselves or in relationships. The inability to relate simply continues; yet they cannot grow spiritually until relating once again resumes.

Children are usually attracted to parents who suffer the exact damage that prevents them from providing a correct situation for the soul of that child. Children who need much physical affection to heal past hurts tend to attract "mental" types of parents who use words to display their affections rather than the critically needed physical contact. Children who need to be taught independence and self-sufficiency to grow spiritually usually find suppressive, interfering parents who stifle any possibility of spiritual growth because of their own unresolved fears.

People cannot grow when they cannot attract relationships and situations that will cause growth. People need the damaged areas of the consciousness healed so they can stop automatically attracting the same hurt and pain. The damages also contain energy. This energy is necessary for growth, and needs to be released so that it can once again be made available to the soul. Using the technology of the Brotherhood (described in Chapter One), distributed through Gentle Wind Retreat, is the fastest way to repair the damage to one's consciousness and to release the potential resources held within these damaged areas.

IDEAS

It is now possible for people to be healed of all past and present life damages by using the technology of the Brotherhood. Such healing will produce profound effects in most people and will prevent people from chronically attracting the same painful situations and relationships that lead nowhere. This healing process will also free the energy stored in the damaged areas of the consciousness, and make this energy once again available for spiritual growth. However, even with damages healed and the energy released, people do not automatically return to a path of evolution. People can only evolve through the correct use of free will. They must still contend with all their normal thoughts, feelings and behavior patterns which do not necessarily support evolution. They must also come to understand the nature and the power of their own ideas. They must come to see that ordinary but incorrect ideas can prevent evolution for thousands of years.

The Age of Darkness leaves humanity burdened with much misinformation. Unraveling this misinformation will take a very long time because people will not want to see how incorrect their ideas actually are. People tend to treasure their ideas and points of view. They do not want to consider the price they pay for holding on to incorrect ideas. Their ideas support their illusions of happiness and their desires to remain comfortable. People have great difficulty sacrificing ideas no matter how much their ideas prevent evolution.

Human ideas of personal happiness are deadly because they rarely correspond to the requirements of the soul. Human ideas of personal happiness are much more aligned with human ego demands for such things as success, power, or relationships. Many people have ideas about what they require in a marriage partner. A woman, for example, might only see herself with a man who looks a certain way or acts a certain way. Perhaps he must have a college education and earn a certain amount of money at some profession that falls within her ideas. He may have to come from a certain kind of family or have certain religious beliefs. The specifications are endless and the idea of the "right" man is very strong.

This woman's idea with all its requirements is only a function of the human personality. The idea has nothing to do with what the soul might require in a companion, and does not question whether the soul even requires a companion. It has nothing to do with finding a partner who likes her, loves her or gives her the support which she needs to evolve. It has nothing to do with whether or not she likes him, loves him or can provide him with what he needs to grow.

When most people say, "I love you," to a potential mate, they are usually saying, "I love how you fit my specifications." They are saying that, "because you fit my specifications, I will be happy." They fail to understand that their specifications are only ideas and that these ideas have nothing to do with happiness. Some people discover that their ideal partners are unfulfilling. Instead of accepting responsibility for their self-made disappointment, they usually blame their partners for this lack of happiness. Others live their lives in comfortable illusions that support their myth of personal happiness. They put their ideal relationship into their ideal home, have some ideal children and surround themselves with comfort and convenience. They live in a world of Hollywood props that keep them standing still. Because the escalator is constantly moving downward, they sink further and further into darkness. Their ideas keep everything too comfortable to produce any change or growth.

Some people have strong ideas about healing that cause a failure to grow. They believe that psychotherapy or some weekend "experience" has healed them. They have ideas about what healing feels like or what constitutes a healing experience. They have specifications and ideas of how spiritual people should look and behave.

They do not understand that a better adjustment into one's damages does not heal the damage. They have no understanding of energy, its uses and its misuses. They think that "feeling good" has something to do with being healed. These are the people who are looking for someone really important to heal them. They want someone "well-known," with a "good reputation." They want their healers to appear powerful or to dress according to their ideas and look like gurus of some sort.

They do not understand that real healing requires a wisdom and a technology that may not be anything like their ideas. They fail to see that genuine healers have no need to be powerful, well-known, or to dress according to some made up idea of what healers look like. Real healers are too busy healing to expend themselves on power, glamour, or reputation. However, many people will cling to their ideas of healing and refuse the real aid necessary to promote their own evolution.

Some people have religious ideas about God, heaven and eternal reward. These are the people who think they can gain heaven by attending Sunday service, regardless of what they might choose to do with their lives. These people simply continue to descend into darkness. It is bad enough that they waste their lives, but they also have strong ideas about heaven and their promised afterlife. So, when they die, they are still looking for their ideas. They refuse to go with the Brothers and Sisters who come for them at physical death. They refuse to go back into the Inner World where they can be properly healed and reeducated. These are the ones who fall into the lower astral planes and wander aimlessly, often clinging to their incorrect ideas while they search for the gates of heaven.

Many people have strong ideas about personal freedom and independence. These ideas are mostly perverted human notions that prevent spiritual growth. These people want to think that they have their own answers and can evolve their own way. They do not want to contemplate that their "answers" are just more human ideas. They cannot see that souls are lost and need the help of the Brotherhood to regain any ability to evolve. They refuse the help and the guidance of the Brotherhood because they do not want their personal notions of freedom and independence threatened. Often, what they are really saying is that they want to be free to continue to hurt themselves, to hurt others and to move further into darkness. They see the Brotherhood as an interference in their own personal plans for happiness.

RESOURCES

This planet has many natural resources including its water supply, minerals, plant life (especially trees for timber), soil, sea life. Some countries are rich in these natural resources while others must import essentials such as certain food products, minerals or fuel. All the world's resources are in the hands of humanity to be used wisely and productively, or to be misused or misspent.

Each human consciousness has certain resources. Some souls are rich in natural resources and have accumulated lifetimes of substance necessary for evolution. Other souls have less available resources. They have either not had ample time in incarnation to gather their energies, or they have simply spent their available energies on something other than evolution. Each in humanity is responsible for his or her individual resources. Each is responsible for accumulating the necessary energy to make the evolutionary climb and to use or spend those energies correctly.

We have already discussed the fact that damages to the consciousness and accompanying behavior patterns can tie up much energy. When the damage is healed, these resources become available to a person again. Since most of humanity suffers from serious damage, much human energy remains trapped in the damage and protective behavior patterns that might potentially be used for evolution. When damages are energetically healed, the potential resources are once again made available to people. However, this healing process alone does not insure evolution. Healing a person of his or her damages does not mean that a person will automatically use the reclaimed resources for spiritual growth. In fact, it is far more probable that these energies will be misused to perpetuate some idea or desire of the human ego structure.

People simply do not understand that they have a limited supply of energy. Each person has only a certain amount. When the human ego has a strong hold on the physical vehicle, that ego uses the available resources to keep the person fulfilling the demands of the ego without regard for the soul. The human ego is more than willing to use the available resources to seek more powerful positions, greater financial gain, more prestige, or "ideal" relationships. The human ego structure rarely cooperates with the requirements of the soul. It uses human will to continue chronic behavior patterns and to cling to human ideas.

We have already discussed the power of human ideas and the fact that people can easily prevent evolution by clinging to an idea such as "personal freedom" or "life everafter." These ideas are powerful, but not because they are correct. Rather, they are powerful because people spend so much energy protecting their incorrect ideas and not acknowledging that these ideas are wrong. Many Catholics, for instance, know that their religion is very dark. They know they have been lied to, abused and misled. They can feel the damage that has been done, but they cannot admit that they were so duped. They do not want to feel stupid. They do not want to look at what they have wasted. So, they protect their Catholic ideas and Catholic positions. They tie up their available resources in protecting what they already know is a huge, empty lie. However, protecting these lies causes them to use their strength and energy to stay the same, to prevent growth. Since the only path of evolution is an escalator moving down, people who protect Catholic lies do not have available energy to climb "up" and only sink further into darkness.

Spiritual growth requires that people use their energies only on behalf of their souls. The climb upward requires great energy and strength. It is a long and difficult climb. To rest is to sink further into darkness. Therefore, one must first have the resources to make the climb and then continuously use those resources on behalf of the soul through acts of spiritual will.

Very few people use their resources for spiritual growth. Most people spend their energies fulfilling their human ideas of personal happiness. People use their resources to get a "good" education or a "good" job. They do not think at all about proper learning for the soul or about doing what the soul requires each day to make a living. They do not realize that by spending their resources on incorrect relationships and painful, or even "comfortable" living situations, they deplete the soul of energy needed to evolve. People do not understand that they cannot easily replenish themselves. In fact, some people have so seriously spent themselves that they need to return to the Inner World through physical death for replenishment. Others are so bankrupt that they literally have nothing left and will have to begin climbing again from some lower point in the animal kingdom.

Some souls have spent their energies striving for spiritual growth. The Age of Darkness, however, has made their climb impossible. It has taken all the energy some souls could muster to climb for thousands of years without support. Some of these souls are spent and need to be replenished. This refueling process most often takes place in the Inner World, but may also take place in incarnation through the help of the Brotherhood. The Brotherhood is more than willing to aid souls who are spent from striving for spiritual growth.

Those who have misused their energies fulfilling the demands of the human ego usually develop patterns of misuse. Often when these people are replenished they continue to misuse their resources lifetime after lifetime because they are caught in their own patterns of misuse. By contrast, those souls "spent" from striving for spiritual growth have usually developed patterns for correct spending and more often correctly use their replenished resources. However, they tend to take difficult approaches to solving problems that could usually be handled with much less expenditure.

Finally, people do not see that each person has a limited amount of time during which resources are actually available. People get energetic help from astrological transits and life situations that are not available at all times. These energies must be used by the soul for evolution during these certain time frames. Otherwise, people must wait until the opportunities and resources roll around again. Some may have to wait for hundreds or even thousands of years.

When a person uses his or her resources for the evolution of the soul, that soul has regeneration ability which is not available to the human ego. Human egos cannot regenerate; they can only spend. Souls, however, can correctly engage themselves in exactly what is required for growth and therefore experience satisfaction and peace. Human egos cannot be satisfied. As a result, they can only drain the consciousness in search of something more or better. Souls can be fulfilled and satisfied. Souls know exactly how to replenish and regenerate once they are on track and how to use all their resources to stay on track. Unless a person is constantly using his or her available energy for continued spiritual growth, he or she is very likely to be misusing that energy and therefore preventing any possible evolution.

CYCLES AND RHYTHMS

People do not yet understand the structure of the mind. They cannot see that each person perceives the world from his or her own unique point of view. Humanity knows very little about inner rhythms and cycles. People do not know why they start things when they do, why they finish things when they do, or why some things never get finished at all. People are so automatic that they rarely understand their own cycles and rhythms. This lack of understanding accounts, in part, for the gross misuse of human resources among so many.

Ironically, people do recognize cycles and rhythms in the lower kingdoms. They know that seeds must be planted at certain times of the year to reap future harvests. They know that to breed animals, they must wait for the animals to be ready, to be "in heat." They know that efforts to plant seeds or breed animals at improper times will simply not yield results.

People are likewise run by their own cycles to a degree, yet the cyclical process itself remains a mystery to most people. Unfortunately, humanity has not yet advanced far enough to properly use a detailed account of human rhythms. However, we do wish to lay the groundwork for a more advanced text and to present people with a simplified version of this information. People need to know that these cycles exist and that each individual person operates within a specific cycle. At this time most people are energetically bound by their own rhythms to a large extent, because the cycle itself is a function of the mind, not the soul, and most people operate completely from the mind.

At the time of birth (give or take three days), each person starts his or her first lunar cycle. The transiting moon governs the individual cycle. In this astrological system, the moon represents the human mind, not the emotions. A lunar cycle lasts 27.53 days, and is called a synodal period. Both men and women have these cycles. These are not menstrual periods, although they are affected by menstrual periods. Women and men have periods. Men actually have "premenstrual" kinds of symptoms and undergo physiological changes. They have changes in their energy level and psychological states. In fact, most men become more aggressive just before and during their "periods." Because aggression is so acceptable and normal for men, humanity does not consider this increase to be a real change. Some men are actually much more psychologically and emotionally imbalanced than women during these "periods." People have developed a whole set of misinformation about menstruation and women that blinds them to the male cycle.

Each person's lunar cycle begins with the exact degree and sign of the sun at the time of birth. This sun sign becomes the exact position of the moon in the lunar cycle. If, for instance, a person was born at 17 degrees of Taurus, then the lunar cycle would begin with the moon at 17 degrees of Taurus. Approximately every 27.53 days from these points, the person enters a new lunar cycle. The sign that introduces the cycle determines the theme of the cycle.

For instance, a person whose lunar cycle begins with a moon in 20 degrees of Taurus, will have the energy to do Taurean kinds of things. He or she will see the world in a Taurean kind of way. This person will be inclined toward activities such as building projects or home repair projects that have a Taurean, earthy quality.

However, it should be understood that the moon cycle in this example begins with 20 degrees of Taurus. Although the moon cycle runs for 27.53 days, the moon will only be in Taurus for the amount of time necessary to travel from 20 degrees to 30 degrees, slightly less than ten days. Then the moon enters the new sign of Gemini. Gemini is a much more mental sign and carries a very different energy and point of view than Taurus.

The person has not entered a new cycle, but has entered a new sign. In entering this sign, this person will not have the benefit of new energy, which is only available at the beginning of a cycle. Therefore, the energy will not be available to start something new. However, the mind has completely shifted gears into Gemini interests, thought patterns, and points of view. The mind has lost its Taurean interest in earthy things. Consequently, the person has probably lost both the interest and the energy to complete any of the Taurean projects that remain.

People know they have the energy and interest for something one day and that it seems to be gone the next. They know that projects sometimes begin easily and then seem to get bogged down and difficult, only they do not understand why. They do not understand that their own inner mind, influenced by the moon, has simply changed the channel to a new program. People are run by their lunar cycles because they rely so heavily on their minds. They are so accustomed to the noise and chatter of the mind, that they do not expect to be quiet inside. As a result, humanity is literally at the mercy of the moving moon.

People in the building trades are good examples of this phenomenon. Plumbers or electricians may contract to do a job on a certain house. They do the job for two or three days and then they disappear for three weeks, leaving the job unfinished. The homeowner may complain and ask for service, but the plumbers and electricians are unconsciously waiting for the moon to cycle back and begin a new cycle. At that point, they will return to the original job, but will literally be starting that job all over again. They are far more successful at completing shorter jobs that fall within an appropriate segment of a given cycle.

In large corporations, jobs get done because there are larger numbers of people doing them. When one person might be waning, someone else is ready to begin. In this way, there are always enough people to keep a project moving and to carry things through. People who usually work alone are much more likely to have difficulty if they are not working with someone who has a complementary cycle. The more people working together in a group, the more likely will a project have the necessary momentum to finish what is started.

People do not understand their own inner clocks, so they do not comprehend when and how much energy is available to them. This system describes the lunar cycle without burdening the reader with mathematical configurations or certain exceptions and individual peculiarities that will be discussed in a future work. Here, we will say that people are relatively bound to the ebb and flow of the lunar cycle. This is not to say that some people cannot force themselves to start a project without the benefit of the energy available at the beginning of a cycle. They can do this. Certain people can also force themselves to finish a project without the real interest or energy needed to complete the job. The problem in both situations is that people are forcing themselves rather than listening to themselves, thus consuming a larger portion of their resources than the given project actually requires. Humanity is destined to be burdened with problems completing things, both individually and collectively, until the mystery of this simple lunar cycle is more readily understood. Again, it should be stated that when the mind is quiet, the consciousness is much less vulnerable to the changes of these rhythms and flows.

THE MALE AND FEMALE EGO STRUCTURE

Each soul must work within the limitations of the human personality and ego structure. The male ego structure can be thought of as a positively charged system. This positive charge causes the male ego structure to more actively seek success, power, or any of the societal symbols of achievement and power. Men are generally programmed and expected to seek power and domination. This does not mean that some women are not similarly programmed, because obviously they are. However, it does mean that males as a group are more constantly and continuously "power" programmed, and that the positively charged system more readily accepts and acts upon the programming.

Males are programmed to seek inner personal feelings of power as well as actual power over the lives of others. Human power is always acquired by assessing the weaknesses of another and then acting in a way that takes advantage of these weaknesses. For example, in most male sports such as football, the idea is to win the game by being able to overtake the other through the use of power. The game involves assessing the weaknesses of the other team, and then developing the proper strategy for using these weaknesses against them.

In football games as well as other sports, "power plays" result in winning the games and pleasing the fans. In human relationships, however, power becomes a much more dangerous kind of programming that often produces disastrous results for men. Men have been trained not only to seek power on the football field, but to use "power plays" as a way of life. Again, this is not to say that some women do not seek power as a way of life, because they do. However, in the positively charged male ego structure, seeking power becomes much more difficult to bring under the control of the soul. Evolution and spiritual growth require the surrendering of human power. Such a surrender is extremely difficult for the male ego structure, making evolution much more difficult for men than it is for women.

The desire for power varies from person to person. Some people have accumulated lifetimes of personal power and have much experience in sustaining power over others that even exists within the soul consciousness. Some people may have hundreds or even thousands of years of domination over others. In the human world, they make excellent lawyers and doctors who use their acquired abilities to continue to succeed in the human sense. Again, when a consciousness already has a history of power and domination and expresses that history in this lifetime as a positively charged male ego structure, the cycle of power accumulation is difficult and nearly impossible to break.

When the male ego structure receives correct spiritual information, the automatic response to this information is often to reject the data and defend against it. If the male ego structure receives information advising that structure to relinquish personal power (so that the energy invested in obtaining power can be used by the soul), the response will be very negative in 90 to 95 percent of all men. The positively charged system responds by being insulted and enraged and continues to cling to its ideas of power. It should also be understood that power and aggression are normal for the positively charged ego system, so that these defensive reactions are extremely normal reactions. Rarely, however, will men be able to get beyond their normal reactions until they acknowledge these responses for what they are, and until they comprehend that they are unable to evolve and keep power at the same time.

Men do not yet understand how much of their personal energies and resources are tied up in seeking and maintaining power. If humanity had access to this energy and could use it for evolution, souls would be moving much faster through the levels and stages of evolution. When men are told by the Brotherhood through a soul reading that they are wasting their resources, most men want to fight that information. Some want to fight the Brotherhood. They are so used to being in charge that they cannot accept help from those who are really in charge of the well-being of this planet.

Men tend to value their own ideas and opinions more than women do. They tend to think they are right because the positively charged system literally feels positive. They misuse their will more often to maintain their ideas and positions, and seek situations that will not threaten their points of view. The work of the Brotherhood is a threat to the male ego structure. Evolution is a threat to this system. People need only look at all the male world leaders to see how the male system operates. None of these so-called leaders care anything about evolution or growth. They represent the worst perversions and distortions of the masculine principle, and reflect the grave problems that this misuse has caused all of humanity.

The female ego structure is a negatively charged system. The female structure is much more familiar with powerlessness and helplessness. Because men have misused their positively charged structures, women have responded to their feelings of powerlessness and helplessness through the "Women's Liberation Movement." These reactions on the part of women are more than understandable. However, these movements have created only more problems for women by causing in them even more distorted and perverted misuses of their own masculine polarity. These women are expressing only their hurts and damages by attempting to cover their wounds with behavior patterns that mimic men. Men are behaving in ways that prevent evolution. Copying these behaviors will never promote evolution and spiritual growth. There is a point in evolution where both men and women must balance their own inner male-female polarities. This cannot be accomplished until women are healed of their damages and are free to live healthy lives as women. In the same way, men must be healed of their damages to begin to live as healthy men.

The female ego structure can more readily surrender human power. It is receptive by nature and therefore receives information from outside its own system with more readiness and much less defensiveness. Women have less difficulty surrendering their own ideas because they do not as readily see these ideas as symbols of their own power. As a group, they receive information from the Brotherhood without as much defensive reaction. They do not tend toward extreme feelings of insult and outrage. They are more able simply to use their energies to work with the information as it is given. They do not tend to distort the information inside themselves. This allows the information to remain more useful to them.

This information has been understood by the "Dark Side" for a long time. It is for this reason that religions are supported by darkness, especially religions that keep men in the dominant roles and refuse to allow women to become leaders. Some religions refuse women equal participation and these are very much supported by the dark ones. In fact, anything controlled by darkness will keep males in the position of dominance and power. The Dark Side will not allow the risk of women becoming powerful and leading people out of darkness. Many governments in the New Age will fall into the hands of women. The government of the Philippines is only the beginning. Women will more readily take information from the Brotherhood and use this information to provide correct leadership. In the human sense, this planet is now run by the male principle— the positively charged, aggressive system. This planet would have much more hope for peace in the hands of the negatively charged, receptive system.

Women should not be fooled into thinking that existing in a female ego structure can automatically produce evolution. This is far from the case. The female ego structure has many misuses to overcome, particularly in the area of glamour. There are gross misuses of sexual energy among women and extreme distortions of the female principle found throughout humanity.

This is simply to say that men must understand that they will have continued, persistent resistance to spiritual growth. If they want to evolve, they must come to understand this normal resistance for what it is and not allow it to prevent them from growing. Women will have much less resistance and will therefore not have to work as much on this particular area.

CHANGE

Throughout this book we have described evolution as a process of growth that requires continuous change. People change every day, but these changes are not necessarily producing evolution. Some people think that psychotherapy or a New Age workshop has helped them change. They conclude that because something has changed, they must be growing. They do not understand that evolution requires a specific kind of change that is both directed and engineered by the individual soul.

When a person "changes" as a result of psychotherapy or some similar experience, these changes are rarely directed by the individual soul. As we have already described, psychotherapy cannot connect the human personality with the soul, and therefore cannot produce evolution. Psychotherapy can help a person develop new chronic behavior patterns that can be used to protect damage. In this sense, a person actually feels that something has been changed. Unfortunately, the "something" that has changed is not anything that can produce evolution. If people could look at themselves through the eyes of the Brotherhood, they would perceive that these "changes" have had absolutely no positive energetic effect on the consciousness. They would see that these people who think they have changed are energetically exactly the same. All of their problems and damages are still in place. The vibration has been unaltered and the soul has no more control over the vehicle than it had before the psychotherapy sessions started.

The same thing is true of any of the New Age workshops and weekend experiences. People are so sure they have changed as a result of these experiences that they lose their ability to see they are still the same. These experiences may cause some people to "feel closer" to others. This feeling may be very pleasant, and may even be temporarily satisfying. However, this feeling will not energetically change a person in the way that is needed for evolution to occur. These changes, again, are not engineered by the soul and cause no soul connection. In some cases "feeling closer" can cause people to absorb energetically the damages and the karma of others. While they think they have "changed" in some positive way, the experience has actually caused negative change. Consequently, people appear more damaged and burdened energetically than before the experience. If they could see themselves through the eyes of the Brotherhood they would observe more dark areas in the consciousness and they would know they had caused themselves only more problems.

People do not understand that the human mind does not have the capacity to engineer and direct the changes required for spiritual growth. Only the soul can implement such change, and this can be done only when the soul has enough connection and control over the human vehicle for this change to be accomplished. Souls, with some exceptions, can engineer and direct the exact kind of change required for evolution. However, change directed by the soul is very subtle and gentle. It is change that does not require force of any kind. Only human change directed by the human ego requires force.

People could think of evolutionary change somewhat like the changing of the seasons. In the springtime, trees know that it is time to bloom. They take their cues from increases in temperature and other environmental factors that trigger the internal programming to begin to bloom. In summer, the same trees become full, green and lush. They automatically grow leaves and fill out and appear very rich. In fall, they slowly change. The greens become yellow, red, orange. The leaves fall off so that by winter, these same trees appear bare and dry.

These trees do not have to "think" about changing. The trees do not "make a decision" to grow in spring or change color in fall. They do not have to discuss, process, or analyze the presence of summer or the coming of winter. They just simply do what trees do. They grow, if properly nourished, without any force whatsoever.

People would not think of hammering on the side of a tree and yelling at it to grow. Yet, they think nothing of attempting to emotionally hammer themselves into changing something about themselves that can only be changed with the help of the soul. People claim to want help with their problems, but they continuously attempt to solve their problems with the human ego. Human egos are too broken and damaged to solve people's problems. Trying to solve problems and produce change through the human ego is like trying to fix a broken machine with a set of broken tools. The job cannot be done.

People expect the trees to change without force, but they do not understand that they too can change without force. This does not mean that people can grow without effort because evolution often requires great effort. Trees expend much energy every day turning sunlight and water into food. They are like self-contained factories that continue to manufacture food for growth. They expend great effort to support their own life functions. This is effort without force. This effort requires only that people stay out of the way and not interfere with the trees' food manufacturing process. Many people have not yet learned to stay out of their own way long enough to let their souls be heard.

There are others who believe that the changes necessary for evolution can occur without effort. This is the opposite side of those who want to use the force of the human ego, and it is just as fruitless. These people tend to believe that someone will come to save them or that someone like Jesus Christ has already accomplished this. They are either waiting for a Messiah or think they can rely on one who lived thousands of years ago. They take no responsibility for their own souls. They sit passively, waiting for someone to make their lives better. Some wait for a New Age guru, or help from beings of other planets. They look up to the sky for the coming of a bright light. They fail to comprehend that their Brothers and Sisters from other worlds and planets cannot help them until they assume responsibility for themselves. They insist on doing nothing. Since the path of evolution is like an escalator moving downward, they cannot stop moving further into darkness because they insist on passively waiting.

Evolution requires change—quiet, subtle and ongoing change. Changes that are engineered by the soul are never forced. People who are evolving find themselves sacrificing the pain and suffering in their lives without thinking about it. They are like the trees changing in the seasons; they are just doing what must be done. When people think they know what to do in order to evolve, they are usually wrong. The part that thinks it knows what to do is only getting in the way of the part that simply does it. When people think they are listening to the voice of the soul, they are almost always listening to the echoes of their own minds, which direct them to change things that have nothing to do with evolution.

At this time, most people cannot hear their own souls, so they have no ability to change in a way that would promote spiritual growth. Those few who might hear their souls have great difficulty listening, because souls need people to change in ways that are not comfortable for people to consider. People do not want to change in ways that would cause them to lose power over others, or prestige, or financial reward. They want to change what they think will benefit the human personality. They do not know that the human ego often naturally resists changes that are engineered by the soul. They do not understand the human nature of this resistance. Instead they see the resistance as a sign that the soul's directive is in some way incorrect.

When people are changing in a way that produces evolution, they rarely like the changes that need to be made. They resist sacrificing painful relationships and hurtful job situations because the human ego wants to keep things the same. When people are growing, they suffer many losses. They may lose old friends, family members and even loved ones who simply cannot support spiritual growth. They can lose prestige, popularity, fame, and wealth because none of these things provide spiritual growth. Very few people will want to change in a way that will produce evolution, because very few people value peace of mind enough to make the difficult changes that evolution requires.

7

THE WAY

THROUGHOUT THIS BOOK, we have described the legacy of darkness that humanity must now face. We have indicated some of the problems that must be solved before evolution can resume. Conditions on this planet are very serious in that people who seek spiritual growth have so little direction and support. Many people are looking for something better, but cannot find the way.

We would say that people must not only find a way, but must locate the Great Way, which is the only possible road to evolution. Most people are like lost travelers who have wandered from their original course, and now cannot find any road signs or maps to direct them back. They are looking for someone who can give them accurate directions, but they continually ask other people who are also lost and in need of aid.

In order to find the Great Way, people must first learn who has the real directions. There are many people who claim to have directions. These are the same ones who claim that there are "many paths" and that they know of one such path. Anyone who thinks there are "many paths" knows absolutely nothing about the Great Way. These people are correct about the existence of "many paths."

However, they do not understand where these paths are actually leading them. They do not realize that these paths are not taking them anywhere in evolution; instead, these paths are actually taking people away from the Great Way.

Those who claim there are "many paths" believe they have found some technique or theory or experience that will cause growth. They rarely evaluate the effectiveness of the technique or theory and often mistake some emotional or psychological event as a "spiritual" experience. These proclaimers know nothing of evolutionary requirements and offer nothing that produces actual growth within the soul. Frequently they use their "discoveries" to become personally powerful, better known, and more successful financially. Their personal lives are travesties and their relationships are filled with pain and suffering. Yet, these are the ones that humanity asks for directions.

Some people have tried many of these "paths." They have attended one workshop after another, searching for something that would bring a longer lasting peace. At times, they might even find some temporary relief in these seminars and experiences. Most often they continue to seek without any real satisfaction or peace, because none of these paths have led them to the Great Way. These seekers are often disappointed in what they find, but they are impelled to go on to a new technique, theory, book, or method that claims to offer growth. And each time they are left disappointed and still seeking, because they have not found the Way.

Each time people start out on one of these "paths," they set their life course in the direction of that path. They use their energies and resources to follow the map they have been given. Usually, they must use much effort and energy attempting to follow these techniques and theories. However, because these "paths" offer nothing for individual souls, they only deplete people's resources without offering any replenishment. Some people have attempted to follow so many of these "paths" that they are almost energetically bankrupt. They are like cars that need to be refueled in order to continue the journey. They insist on driving without first making sure they have chosen a route with plenty of service stations at regular intervals. They do not watch the gas gauge, nor do they understand that it is possible to use up their resources following incorrect directions from other lost people.

Some people think they know who has the proper directions. These are the ones who have strong mental ideas and pictures of what a guru or teacher would be like. Some people think that teachers should be well-educated, powerful and well-known. They fail to see that education, power and prestige are usually signs that a person is not involved in spiritual evolution, but rather is using his or her resources to perpetuate the longings and demands of the human ego. Souls do not seek human power and prestige, nor are they interested in higher education. These mental ideas cause people to follow those who are not going anywhere in evolution. To choose a teacher who is not growing is to remain in darkness, falling farther down the evolutionary ladder.

Some people think their gurus and teachers should look, act or dress a certain way. Many think that gurus wear beards, Indian style clothing, robes and turbans. They are looking for accents and profound mental teachings. Some want psychic phenomena or mediumship. They want all the right props and accoutrements. Usually, that is exactly what they find—props, robes, and mind tricks. They do not find evolution.

Those with strong mental ideas find "paths" that are full of other mental ideas. They find ideas about meditation, evolution and growth. They are not looking with their hearts. They are looking only with their minds. Human minds are filled with misinformation and endless supplies of mental junk. It is true that ideas are necessary to function in the physical world. It is also true, however, that the human mind is completely incapable of producing any evolution. It is too busy and too filled with mediocrity to produce anything for the soul. People who look for evolution with their minds find only mediocrity and mental junk. They cannot find the Great Way. The road of evolution is quiet and still, without the clanking of mind ideas. The Great Way is a road traveled from the heart.

Sadly, many who read this work will think they have found another "path." They are so addicted to searching that they will not recognize what they have found. They are so involved in their tiny but busy mental worlds that they will pass by the entrance to the Great Way while looking for the way.

CHOOSING A TEACHER

In order to travel on the Way of evolution, people must abide by the rules of the road. Spiritual law requires that each soul find his or her own teacher. Each soul must find someone who is evolving and follow that someone up the ladder of Hierarchy. Everyone has a place on the ladder. Each soul is responsible for following the one he or she has chosen as a teacher. Additionally, each soul must lead the way up the ladder for any other souls who will listen and follow.

Hierarchy could be thought of as levels or steps in evolution. Each level represents a higher quality of life and an increased awareness or vibration. The entire planet has been set up according to hierarchy. Vibrations or levels of existence range from the very dense vibration of the mineral, vegetable and lower animal kingdoms to very high states of consciousness—too high for humanity to comprehend or even imagine. Souls are automatically working their way up the ladder of Hierarchy. They are automatically following the person in front of them on the ladder.

If a person chooses a "teacher" who knows nothing of the Great Way, they are simply following someone into darkness. We have already described some of the unfortunate, misguided ideas that cause people to make poor choices when searching for spiritual guidance. The aftermath of darkness has left people unable to grow without genuine guidance. People cannot find this guidance in the physical world. They must look to the nonphysical world for help.

In order for people to evolve at this time, they must establish a connection with a seventh degree initiate. Seventh degree initiates have accumulated the necessary spiritual knowledge and information to help people evolve. There are only a handful of seventh degree initiates now in physical bodies. They cannot make themselves known because people are not ready to be taught. Furthermore, a seventh degree initiate could not be subjected to the vibration of most of humanity. The likelihood of finding one of these few souls is extremely limited. These initiates are well-hidden and are not on this planet for the purpose of public teaching. If a person had actually connected with a teacher at this level, he or she would definitely not be reading this material. In fact, if someone was already connected with a seventh degree initiate, that person would simply be following the teacher without any need to search for this kind of information.

People must look, then, to the Inner World to find their teachers. However, people do not want to accept the reality of the nonphysical world. People are taught to believe only in those things they can know with their five senses. They are taught to believe in the "scientific method" and to look for "scientific proof" before accepting information as accurate. They do not want to acknowledge that science, as humanity knows it, is darkness without any light. Science prevents people from knowing the reality of their own souls. It causes people to direct their energies into the dense, physical world that can be seen, heard, felt, tasted, and smelled, while avoiding the real world of evolution and growth.

People attempt to apply the scientific method when choosing a teacher. They want someone they can see and hear, regardless of whether or not that someone is providing accurate spiritual information. They would rather listen to ministers, priests, rabbis, and New Age gurus than to Inner World souls who can provide them with the necessary connection to a seventh degree initiate. Over 98 percent of this planet's "spiritual leaders" are uninitiated souls. They often hold a much lower vibration than those seeking their leadership. Many people actually lower their own vibrations in order to follow their so-called leaders.

People must also understand the structure and the function of Planetary Hierarchy. As has been stated, Hierarchy can best be described as levels of existence. These levels are connected in a very logical order and were established by spiritual law. The order of Hierarchy cannot be violated. This means that first degree initiates do not directly connect to seventh degree initiates. The great discrepancy in vibration would prevent both from benefiting by such a relationship in a way that could promote evolution. It is much more likely that a first degree initiate would connect to a third degree initiate who might connect to a fourth or fifth degree initiate who then might connect to a seventh degree initiate.

There are very few seventh degree initiates even in the Inner World. There are a few more sixth degree initiates, and even more fifth degree initiates. There are thousands and thousands of third and fourth degree initiates, and even thousands more second degree initiates. It is therefore much easier to find a third or fourth degree initiate to follow who can connect the person to the source of spiritual guidance that is necessary for evolution to take place.

There are third and fourth degree initiates who have broken from their own teachers and are out doing their own thing. They have lost the protection of the Brotherhood and are no longer evolving under the shield. They have very little or no ability to promote anyone else's evolution because they have broken from the source of their own spiritual guidance. People will see these renegades fall from their positions because they become subject to public exposure when they lose the protection of the shield.

People do not understand that the reason they must choose their own teachers is that they must follow someone up the ladder of Hierarchy. They do not see that some of their teachers are like stalled out cars on the highway. The cars are too broken down to move, and the traffic is backed up for miles behind them. People must discover for themselves whether they are actually moving or stalled out behind someone who did not know where he or she was going in the first place. To find evolution and the necessary guidance to accomplish spiritual growth, people will have to accept help from the nonphysical world. They will have to choose souls who are moving and growing. They will have to stop trying to drive behind stalled souls who are not going anywhere, even if they look and sound like true teachers. No spiritual movement is possible until a soul finds someone to follow who knows the Way and is dedicated to traveling this single evolutionary route.

When people establish a connection between themselves and the Brotherhood, they have made the necessary connection with a seventh degree initiate, even though they may not be in direct contact. People must be certain, however, that the ones who claim to be connected with the Brotherhood have actually established such a connection. Evolving under the shield of the Brotherhood is the only safe way to grow, and is by far the most efficient means of spiritual evolution.

PERSONAL SACRIFICE

For evolution to occur, people must be willing to make many personal sacrifices. Often, however, people do not understand what needs to be sacrificed or why such a sacrifice must be made. The sacrifices required for evolution include anything that robs the soul of needed energy and causes the soul to be without the resources to pull itself up the ladder. Because people attempt to grow through the use of human ego and mind, they rarely make sacrifices. And those they do make are, in most instances, incorrect and useless.

Christians, especially Catholics, think that Jesus sacrificed himself on the cross as an example of personal sacrifice and as an act of redemption for all of humanity. They tell themselves that "Jesus died for our sins," and that "Jesus saves." Jesus did not die for anyone. He gave up his physical life in order to complete his personal requirements for the fourth initiation. At that time, physical death was the only way he could move from the third level to the fourth. Jesus raised only his own vibration. His relinquishment of the physical body did absolutely nothing for anyone's soul but his own.

People carry a misinformed view of Jesus' life which causes them to make either incorrect sacrifices or none at all. Those who make incorrect sacrifices believe that giving up sweets for lent, or eating only certain foods, will cause spiritual growth. These are the ones who believe that to endure personal pain as Jesus endured pain on the cross is to cause evolution. They are the ones who sacrifice their personal well-being "for the sake of the children" and stay married to alcoholic spouses in the name of being a "good Christian." They are fools because evolution is never accomplished through the continuation of personal pain. Evolution is never accomplished through acts of personal martyrdom. It is accomplished only through an increased sense of well-being and inner peace. In a sense, well-being is the only sacrifice an evolving soul must never make. Yet, it is the sacrifice that churches encourage and religions demand.

Then, there are those who even more foolishly think that Jesus died for them, leaving them free to do anything they want. They believe they have already been saved, and all that is necessary is prayer. They make none of the sacrifices required for spiritual growth. They are also the ones who believe that a "Savior" will come again to redeem humanity. They sit passively waiting for the new Messiah, or for the Space Brothers to come with the technology to save humanity. Ironically, as long as people hold such irresponsible attitudes, the Brotherhood cannot send in the help that a genuine spiritual leader could offer, nor can humanity obtain aid from their Brothers and Sisters from other planetary bodies.

Evolution requires first that people look at the areas of their lives that cause them continued pain and suffering. Chronic pain and suffering consume a great portion of human energy that could be used for spiritual growth. Yet, people become addicted to their own hurt. Many suffer from chronic pain but do not know how badly they are hurting, or how much energy they are actually using to cope with the pain. It is as though some people have a very bad toothache. They have had the toothache for so long that they have forgotten they even have it. They have adjusted to the toothache and have geared all their systems to coping with the pain. They do not realize how much better they would feel if the toothache was fixed; that is, if they cleaned up the area of their life that was causing the chronic hurt and pain.

The Brotherhood has provided humanity with a healing technology that will alleviate the energetic sources of pain. This technology is available to all of humanity and is distributed only through Gentle Wind Retreat. However, many people refuse to use the technology, often because they cannot imagine living without their familiar toothaches. Some use the instruments, but insist on remaining in the relationships and situations that will cause the pain to come back.

The Brotherhood can and will continue to provide healing instruments that will improve the quality of people's lives. However, through acts of free will people must sacrifice the situations that cause them pain. Evolution is not possible without these sacrifices because the energy required for growth is being used to cope with the chronic pain.

People must also learn to sacrifice the chronic behavior patterns they have developed to protect the pain. If a person actually had a perpetual toothache, that person would learn to adjust to the pain with certain coping behaviors. He or she might discover ways to eat more carefully, using only certain teeth and eating only certain foods. Finally, all of the eating habits would be designed to protect the toothache from becoming more painful. People do the same thing with painful life situations. They develop behavior patterns that protect their original hurts from becoming more painful. People, for example, develop patterns that promote glamour or personal appearance. They develop behaviors that cause them to remain in control, to have power over others, or to always appear successful. They learn to be "one up" on others or to live always in the "one down" position. These behavior patterns consume much human energy and prevent people from living and relating in natural, healthy ways.

The healing instruments of the Brotherhood can heal the original sources of the pain, but they cannot alter the chronic behavior patterns developed to protect the pain. Once healed of damages, the soul will naturally attract situations that offer opportunities to learn new ways of behaving and relating. Nevertheless, chronic behavior patterns are sacrificed only through an act of free will. People cannot evolve and still maintain these patterns because the patterns simply consume the resources needed by the soul in order to grow.

People must learn to sacrifice ideas, particularly ideas about personal happiness. People do need to have certain ideas in order to function in the physical universe. They need to hold on to certain ideas to maintain equilibrium. However, some people have very strong ideas about what will make them happy. Many times these are the ones who are preoccupied with their own personal comfort and convenience. They seek their "ideas" in personal relationships and want to live only with ideal marriage partners. They use most of their available energy to continue their ideas of comfort and convenience. They use their resources to prevent themselves from changing or undergoing any discomfort that would produce evolution. They are dedicated to keeping things the same while their souls require ongoing change in order to grow.

Ideas are very difficult to sacrifice. People become quite fond of their own ideas and they want to be right about things. They do not want to admit they are wrong or to see what their precious ideas are costing them. They are not inclined to make sacrifices of any kind in the area of their own ideas.

THE SEARCH FOR PERFECTION

Evolution is ultimately a search for perfection. This perfection, though, has nothing to do with the human concepts and ideas of perfection. People try to be perfect at doing the wrong things for the wrong reasons. They attempt to find perfect relationships when no such relationships exist. They look for perfect jobs when there are none to be found. They are chronically looking in all the wrong places for a kind of perfection that can be accomplished only through the soul.

People are trained to be "perfect" from the time they begin formal education. Even the early years of education are spent trying to avoid any mistakes. Schools punish students who make mistakes. To succeed in school, children must avoid making errors. They must work to get "good grades," which can be accomplished only through avoiding mistakes. They must try to be perfect at things that have no real meaning and in subjects that have no spiritual value.

Grading systems reward students who can avoid making mistakes while punishing students who make errors. Teachers generally have more positive attitudes toward children who achieve good grades. Teachers have contempt toward children who make errors, and often humiliate them for doing so. In parochial school systems, nuns and priests have a unique way of causing students to feel that a mistake is irreparable. They treat errors in math or spelling as though they were sins against God. They use their "religious" positions to frighten children when they make mistakes, causing children much harm through humiliation and negative emotional responses. Children taught by nuns and priests fear making errors as though these normal errors would incur punishment from God.

People, then, go on to apply these endarkened educational ideas to life situations. They seek to find perfect marriage partners as though someone would be grading them on the subject of marriage. They protect their marital problems and hide their difficulties so that no one will think they have made a mistake. They rarely solve normal relationship problems in healthy ways because they are too busy covering up the problems.

People try to be perfect parents. They have completely incorrect ideas about proper parenting. Worse than that, they try to live up to these incorrect ideas by doing all the "right" things. They expect things from their children that their children often cannot produce. They even want their children to be perfect so they can think of themselves as perfect parents. They do not wish to admit that their ideas are incorrect, nor do they want to consider how many errors they have actually made. They rarely solve the natural problems inherent in parent-child relationships because they are too busy protecting their ideas of perfect parenting. They know nothing about the spiritual and emotional needs of their children because they are too occupied with creating "perfect children" who will support their incorrect ideas of perfect parenting.

Evolution cannot occur unless people can safely make mistakes.

Human beings can learn solely through trial and error. Human beings can gain knowledge only by making mistakes. People can evolve only in situations that not only allow errors, but support and celebrate errors as opportunities to learn.

Souls who seek spiritual growth are seeking a kind of perfection. That perfection is nothing like the standard of perfection offered by education, nor is it related to human ideas of perfection that plague human relationships, causing much unnecessary suffering and pain. Souls are seeking perfection through growth. Each soul sets its own individual standard of perfection. Each soul must upgrade those individual standards of perfection according to the level of spiritual accomplishment.

Human egos set standards of perfection based upon external standards and realities. School children, for example, pursue good grades because good grades reflect an external standard of perfection. Souls, however, always set their own internal standards. These internal standards have nothing to do with anyone else. They have to do only with the personal spiritual accomplishment of that individual soul. Souls have no need to compete for good grades or to achieve over another. Souls are interested exclusively in accomplishing the spiritual requirements necessary for ongoing evolution.

At each level of evolution, souls must establish a standard of perfection consistent with that level. A first degree initiate's requirements for perfection are very different from the requirements of a fourth degree initiate. In the spiritual world, no standard of perfection is considered to be any better than another.

Although the actual accomplishment of perfection occurs within the soul, people must express their individual perfection out into the physical world through some creative act. As souls move upward, people must have access to physical world situations and equipment that allow them to continuously express the inner standard of perfection. People must be able to make things out of wood, metal, or some other substance. They must be able to create through writing, photography, woodworking, welding—some physical representation of their own ongoing spiritual growth. In fact, the physical world exists so that people can use the external world to continuously express inner perfection and growth.

The Age of Darkness has caused people to lose sight of their own inner standards for spiritual perfection, and to waste their energies attempting to respond to external standards and systems that have no meaning for the soul. Darkness has caused people much pain, humiliation and embarrassment when they have made errors that could potentially produce spiritual growth. Until people can make mistakes with inner acceptance and outer support from others, evolution will be greatly suppressed because souls simply cannot grow without mistakes. Nor can people evolve in a world that fails to provide them with the correct avenues to continuously express their inner accomplishment and growth.

BALANCE

The Great Way is a very narrow road that demands the continued focus and attention of its travelers. Under current evolutionary conditions, the Way is more like a tightrope that can be walked only by those who travel with great care and vigilance. The longer a person travels on this road, the narrower it becomes, until life must be lived on the razor's edge.

Walking the road of evolution requires emotional and mental balance. Balance is very difficult to maintain in an imbalanced world. Many of the recent healing instruments offered to humanity by the Brotherhood are energetically designed to bring people into a state of balance. Evolution requires an inner peace and quiet; otherwise, a person cannot hear the voice of his or her own soul. Using these healing instruments on a regular basis can help a person maintain a sense of equilibrium and inner quiet.

Again, using the instruments will not automatically insure perpetual balance. It would be impossible for most people always to remain in balance while living in a world that is extremely out of balance. Even in the course of healthy lives it is normal for people to be thrown out of balance either by their own inner thoughts and feelings or by some event in the external environment. However, it is also normal for people to remain out of balance for very long periods of time. Some people have lived out of balance for hundreds and even thousands of years.

The Brotherhood offers a healing technology that can return the consciousness to a state of balance in a matter of minutes if used as directed. Unfortunately, people do not yet understand the importance of being responsible for their own inner equilibrium. Usually, they do not even know when they are out of balance. Even people who own healing instruments cannot remember or do not know when to use them because they have developed so many automatic responses to being out of balance.

Emotional and mental peace are critical for those who want to grow. Yet, people do not know what it means to be at peace. They know their lives are chaotic and overwhelming. Some of them refer to their imbalances as "stress." Humanity has developed many incorrect ideas about stress and so-called stress reduction. People are willing to pay large fees for stress seminars and exercise programs that claim to offer relief. These programs do absolutely nothing to bring a person back into balance. Stress programs are designed so that people can continue to live unhealthy lives in unhealthy relationships by developing more suitable coping mechanisms.

Some people try to meditate to combat stress while others attempt to exercise their imbalances away. Although meditation may provide some calm, it cannot return the consciousness to a balanced state except under very rare circumstances. Most of today's runners are literally running away from situations in their lives that cause them personal pain which they refuse to acknowledge. No evolution or growth occurs at any stress clinics or in stress reduction seminars or groups. These are expensive and useless methods of coping with imbalanced lives.

Many physical symptoms and problems can be traced to system imbalances. Physicians, for example, have had much difficulty isolating and curing the source of the common cold. Part of the difficulty in treating cold symptoms is that the symptoms are often caused by imbalances rather than viruses. Treatment, therefore, becomes very difficult due to medicine not yet understanding the human consciousness.

People suffer many unnecessary diseases that begin as imbalances. When an imbalance remains uncorrected for a long period of time, the whole system becomes weakened as a result of working much harder to survive in a state of imbalance. Medicine is beginning to detect that some diseases are preceded by traumatic emotional events. For instance, some scientists have noticed that many cancer patients suffered painful losses prior to the onset of the disease. Often, this painful emotional event has thrown the system into such great imbalance that the physical body becomes much more vulnerable to disease. We will save further discussion about the proper energetic care and treatment of the physical vehicle for another book. Here we will simply repeat that uncorrected system imbalances can lead to unnecessary physical problems that have nothing to do with evolution.

People are accustomed to living in emotional and mental imbalance. Many psychotherapy techniques actually teach people to hurl themselves into their emotions through screaming, yelling, or wailing. Psychotherapists believe that "expressing" feelings can restore mental health. Nothing could be further from the truth. People do not go into balance by hurling themselves into their emotions. Nor do they find balance by stuffing or hiding their normal feelings. Natural emotion occurs when people are in a state of balance. In times of emotional crisis people would be aided to a far greater degree by holding a healing instrument offered by the Brotherhood. They would return to a state of balance and thus allow their systems to determine what would be natural expressions of any given emotion.

People do not yet realize that the human ego exists in polarities. What goes up, comes down. If they insist on leading high-pitched, exciting lives, they will also have to experience the lows and the depressions. Some people would find a more balanced life very boring. They do not understand the energy that is wasted in swinging between the ups and the downs. Those who prefer to continue swinging will not be interested in traveling the Great Way, and should wait until they want inner peace as much as they now want to swing with their emotions.

We have referred to the healing instruments of the Brotherhood because these instruments offer humanity the most efficient and effective means of maintaining inner balance and peace. If the conditions on this planet were more conducive to evolution, such instruments might not be necessary. However, present conditions make evolution nearly impossible. Some people will complain that they would prefer not to be dependent on a healing instrument to maintain their equilibrium. These are the ones who would prefer to depend upon their own ideas, or on humanity's common solutions such as drugs, alcohol, exercise, or therapy, none of which promotes spiritual growth. People cannot evolve unless they are continually brought back into a state of balance and calm. The technology of the Brotherhood offers humanity the possibility of evolution at a time when growth would be otherwise impossible.

HIERARCHY: THE INNER WORLD

Throughout this work, we have said that people must evolve up through the levels or stages of existence known as Planetary Hierarchy. We have spoken of the fact that hierarchy exists in the physical world as well as the Inner World, or nonphysical world. Hierarchy is the Great Way and the only way. People can readily observe the levels of existence in the physical world because the physical world is dense and visible. They cannot observe the levels of existence in the nonphysical world because the Inner World is less dense and is visible only to those few people with etheric vision. Even with etheric vision, people could not see the Inner World past a certain vibration, depending on their own level of evolution.

People have confused ideas about the Inner World and the Brotherhood. Many religions teach misinformation about the existence of heaven, hell, purgatory, and offer other afterlife illusions that are inaccurate and simply do not exist. People are also filled with misinformation as a result of science fiction movies and books that describe planets and places where life is eternal. These science fiction accounts are usually more accurate than religious ideas of afterlife, but they still mislead souls to expect bizarre or strange occurrences at death that do not take place.

We have spoken about the Brotherhood throughout this book and of the fact that this work is channelled directly to humanity from the Brotherhood. We have described ourselves as a group of Inner World souls who are dedicated to the evolution of humanity. When people hear and think of the Brotherhood, they conjure up false images and misinformation. They think of physical world clubs and organizations, some that help people and some that actually do harm. People react to the masculine gender and want to know why not the Sisterhood, or the Brotherhood and Sisterhood. They think in human physical world terms and then attempt to apply these physical world ideas to the nonphysical Inner World.

The nonphysical world has many representations in the physical world. Clubs and organizations actually are a physical world representation of the Brotherhood, for example. However, when something from the Inner World is expressed through the human ego with all the accompanying damage, those expressions are usually distorted or perverted representations of life in the Inner World. Physical world clubs are generally without purpose. Physical world organizations such as religious groups are dedicated to darkness. The Brotherhood is a club that exists only for the purpose of evolution. It is an organization of souls completely dedicated to that which is light.

The same thing is true of Inner World government. This planet and all others are governed by Planetary Hierarchy. The physical world reflects but distorts the principles of hierarchical government. In the physical world, people seek power over others so that they can obtain and amass that power for themselves. World leaders seek prestige and fame, again for their own personal gain. Very few physical world leaders care anything about the people they claim to want to lead. Governments generally attract leaders with past life histories that are very dark. Often, these officials have had lifetimes of lying, cheating, stealing, murdering, raping and pillaging. People need only look at those countries where the now-exiled leaders once robbed their impoverished people of millions of dollars out of bottomless greed and avarice. These leaders, to this day, care nothing for their people. Nor do they feel any remorse for the hundreds of thousands of lives that were negatively affected by their desires for wealth. The truth is that nearly every government in the world has been founded on darkness. In government, wearing a suit and looking dapper is usually a cover for a consciousness completely dedicated to itself without concern for others.

The nonphysical world government has no need to accumulate power. Those souls who hold leadership positions do so because they have given up all human ideas and desires for power. Spiritual laws are based only on the best interest of all souls and are upheld by Inner World beings who want only to serve humanity. These spiritual leaders do not want to take anything from people, but want only to give people the things they need for evolution and growth.

People cannot comprehend that Hierarchy treats all souls as royal princes and princesses, and wants only the best for each soul in humanity. Humanity cannot comprehend that the Inner World souls work night and day to help those in the physical and lower astral planes find peace. Many people do not even return to the Inner World at physical death because they cannot comprehend the kind of help and support being offered.

The Inner World is filled with real beauty. There is no need for glamour. Glamour is the physical world substitute for real beauty. People are preoccupied with their physical appearance because they do not understand that real beauty exists in the nonphysical world. They cannot comprehend that the physical body is more like a transportation vehicle for the soul.

The Inner World is filled with peace. The outer world is filled with chaos and excitement. People say they are looking for peace, but they are more often looking for chaos, excitement, and thrills. They want loud music, bright lights, flashy colors, and a fast pace. They find peace boring because they are so addicted to excitement. They cannot imagine that a peaceful world exists anywhere, because they are so hooked on all the noise.

The promise of the New Age is that the outer world—the evolutionary plane—will once again be restored. This means that the physical world will accurately reflect the nonphysical world. It means that life will have purpose and that world leaders will want only to serve. It means that glamour will be replaced by real beauty and that chaos will give way to peace. The Brotherhood and Planetary Hierarchy pledge to remain with humanity until this mission is accomplished.

CONCLUSION

This book is the beginning of many volumes of information about the nature of evolution and the spiritual restoration that must be accomplished. This work is an introduction to the idea and the realities of spiritual growth. It is offered at this time to help humanity correct misinformed ideas and to begin to see themselves as souls instead of bodies and minds. This book, and the others to follow, are offered so that people can awaken to the darkness and stagnation that has besieged this planet. It is understood that awakening from the long sleep of endarkenment will be a jolt and a shock for some. It is understood that people will initially resist such information because it confronts the very foundation of human life. Neverthe-less, it is the hope of the Brotherhood that this foundation can be shaken and that this turbulence will cause present structures to fall. There is no other way to bring about the necessary changes in people and in life on this planet.

The book comes at this time because the present planetary ener-gies are demanding that people change. Astrologically, we are en-tering the Age of Aquarius, a period of about two thousand years that will be strongly influenced by the planet Uranus. The transi-tional period from one astrological age to another always brings about some confusion, chaos and opportunity for change. Uranus brings disruption and collapse by its nature, so this particular tran-sition will be marked by planetary turbulence and disorder. Uranus energetically shakes the foundation of any established system whether that system is an entire government or an individual set of ideas. Furthermore, Uranus tends to deliver this turmoil in abrupt and unexpected ways. If the system or the ideas can withstand the test of Uranus, the system is probably constructed on a solid, stable foundation that can withstand the test of time.

Most human systems are constructed on lies, illusions and dark-ness. People can already see the chaos and confusion erupting in many countries throughout the world. Corrupt world leaders and endarkened forms of government are already beginning to collapse. Economic systems are being tested. Social problems of poverty and homelessness are becoming more evident. People are beginning to challenge physicians, lawyers, and public servants to respond to their needs. Even changes and shifts in the physical planet will bring about increased natural disasters, volcanoes, earthquakes, and unusual weather patterns.

The same kind of disruptive energies will cause changes in in-dividual people. People will be energetically forced to look at their lives, beliefs, and values. Uranus will shake the foundation of their ideas and life positions in order to ferret out those ideas and patterns that are useless and outdated. For some, this energy will be an ongoing nuisance causing them to develop new lies and illusions to cover up the reality that the old way is not working. For others, however, Uranus will bring the energy needed to collapse the inner structures that now prevent evolution.

These changes and disruptions are already destined to occur. The

Brotherhood offers this work at this time for those who wish to reconstruct their lives on truth and reality, free of lies and illusions that prevent growth. This work is offered for those who know in their hearts that things, both on this planet and in their personal lives, are not right. It is for those who are willing to look at how "not right" things are and to take responsibility for beginning the necessary changes.

People can grow only when they can see and say that the emperor is naked; otherwise all available energy is spent pretending he is dressed. People cannot make changes in either their individual lives or the conditions on this planet until they see the reality of darkness that now exists. The Brotherhood offers this work to shed light on what is now very black. Future books will also be written to supply much-needed light. However, humanity must decide whether to keep the light alive and spreading, or to once again snuff out the hope of spiritual growth with more lies, illusions and darkness. The choice belongs to humanity.

WITH IGNORANCE

Also by C. K. Williams

Lies
I Am the Bitter Name
Women of Trachis (translation), with Gregory Dickerson

C. K. Williams

WITH IGNORANCE

HOUGHTON MIFFLIN COMPANY BOSTON
1977

This work was completed with the help of a grant
from the John Simon Guggenheim Memorial Foundation.

Some of these poems have appeared in the following
publications: "Toil" and "The Shade" in *The
New Yorker*. "Spit," "The Last Deaths," "The
Sanctity," "Hog Heaven," and "Blades" in
The American Poetry Review. "The Cave" was
published in a substantially different version in
The Chicago Review.

Library of Congress Cataloging in Publication Data
Williams, Charles Kenneth, date
With ignorance. I. Title.
PS3673.I4483W5   811'.5'4   76–58516
ISBN 0–395–25342–X   ISBN 0–395–25339–X pbk.

Printed in the United States of America

W 10 9 8 7 6 5 4 3 2 1

à
Catherine,
tout

Contents

WITH IGNORANCE

The Sanctity

FOR NICK AND ARLENE DE CREDICO

The men working on the building going up here have got these great,
little motorized wheelbarrows that're supposed to be for lugging bricks and mortar
but that they seem to spend most of their time barrel-assing up the street in,
racing each other or trying to con the local secretaries into taking rides in the
    bucket.
I used to work on jobs like that and now when I pass by the skeleton of the
    girders
and the tangled heaps of translucent brick wrappings, I remember the guys I was
    with then
and how hard they were to know. Some of them would be so good to be with at
    work,
slamming things around, playing practical jokes, laughing all the time, but they
    could be miserable,
touchy and sullen, always ready to imagine an insult or get into a fight anywhere
    else.
If something went wrong, if a compressor blew or a truck backed over somebody,
they'd be the first ones to risk their lives dragging you out
but later you'd see them and they'd be drunk, looking for trouble, almost
    murderous,
and it would be frightening trying to figure out which person they really were.
Once I went home to dinner with a carpenter who'd taken me under his wing
and was keeping everyone off my back while he helped me. He was beautiful but
    at his house, he sulked.
After dinner, he and the kids and I were watching television while his wife
    washed the dishes

and his mother, who lived with them, sat at the table holding a big cantaloupe in
  her lap,
fondling it and staring at it with the kind of intensity people usually only look
  into fires with.
The wife kept trying to take it away from her but the old lady squawked
and my friend said, "Leave her alone, will you?" "But she's doing it on purpose,"
  the wife said.
I was watching. The mother put both her hands on it then, with her thumbs
  spread
as though the melon were a head and her thumbs were covering the eyes and she
  was aiming it like a gun or a camera.
Suddenly the wife muttered, "You bitch!" ran over to the bookshelf, took a book
  down —
A History of Revolutions — rattled through the pages and triumphantly handed it
  to her husband.
A photograph: someone who's been garroted and the executioner, standing behind
  him in a business hat,
has his thumbs just like that over the person's eyes, straightening the head,
so that you thought the thumbs were going to move away because they were only
  pointing
the person at something they wanted him to see and the one with the hands was
  going to say, "Look! Right there!"
"I told you," the wife said. "I swear to god she's trying to drive me crazy."
I didn't know what it all meant but my friend went wild, started breaking things,
  I went home
and when I saw him the next morning at breakfast he acted as though nothing had
  happened.
We used to eat at the Westfield truck stop, but I remember Fritz's, The Victory,
  The Eagle,
and I think I've never had as much contentment as I did then, before work, the
  light just up,
everyone sipping their coffee out of the heavy white cups and teasing the
  middle-aged waitresses
who always acted vaguely in love with whoever was on jobs around there right
  then

besides the regular farmers on their way back from the markets and the long-haul
  truckers.
Listen: sometimes when you go to speak about life it's as though your mouth's
  full of nails
but other times it's so easy that it's ridiculous to even bother.
The eggs and the toast could fly out of the plates and it wouldn't matter
and the bubbles in the level could blow sky high and it still wouldn't.
Listen to the back-hoes gearing up and the shouts and somebody cracking his
  sledge into the mortar pan.
Listen again. He'll do it all day if you want him to. Listen again.

Spit

*. . . then the son of the "superior race" began to spit into the Rabbi's mouth
so that the Rabbi could continue to spit on the Torah . . .*

THE BLACK BOOK

After this much time, it's still impossible. The SS man with his stiff hair and his
    uniform;
the Rabbi, probably in a torn overcoat, probably with a stained beard the other
    would be clutching;
the Torah, God's word, on the altar, the letters blurring under the blended
    phlegm;
the Rabbi's parched mouth, the SS man perfectly absorbed, obsessed with perfect
    humiliation.
So many years and what is there to say still about the soldiers waiting impatiently
    in the snow,
about the one stamping his feet, thinking, "Kill him! Get it over with!"
while back there the lips of the Rabbi and the other would have brushed
and if time had stopped you would have thought they were lovers,
so lightly kissing, the sharp, luger hand under the dear chin,
the eyes furled slightly and then when it started again the eyelashes of both
    of them
shyly fluttering as wonderfully as the pulse of a baby.
Maybe we don't have to speak of it at all, it's still the same.
War, that happens and stops happening but is always somehow right there,
    twisting and hardening us;
then what we make of God — words, spit, degradation, murder, shame; every
    conceivable torment.
All these ways to live that have something to do with how we live
and that we're almost ashamed to use as metaphors for what goes on in us
but that we do anyway, so that love is battle and we watch ourselves in love

become maddened with pride and incompletion, and God is what it is when we're
    alone
wrestling with solitude and everything speaking in our souls turns against us like
    His fury
and just facing another person, there is so much terror and hatred that yes,
spitting in someone's mouth, trying to make him defile his own meaning,
would signify the struggle to survive each other and what we'll enact to
    accomplish it.

There's another legend.
It's about Moses, that when they first brought him as a child before Pharaoh,
the king tested him by putting a diamond and a live coal in front of him
and Moses picked up the red ember and popped it into his mouth
so for the rest of his life he was tongue-tied and Aaron had to speak for him.
What must his scarred tongue have felt like in his mouth?
It must have been like always carrying something there that weighed too much,
something leathery and dead whose greatest gravity was to loll out like an ox's,
and when it moved, it must have been like a thick embryo slowly coming alive,
butting itself against the inner sides of his teeth and cheeks.
And when God burned in the bush, how could he not cleave to him?
How could he not know that all of us were on fire and that every word we said
    would burn forever,
in pain, unquenchably, and that God knew it, too, and would say nothing Himself
    ever again beyond this,
ever, but would only live in the flesh that we use like firewood,
in all the caves of the body, the gut cave, the speech cave:
He would slobber and howl like something just barely a man that beats itself
    again and again onto the dark,
moist walls away from the light, away from whatever would be light for this last
    eternity.
"Now therefore go," He said, "and I will be with thy mouth."

Toil

After the argument — argument? battle, war, harrowing; you need shrieks, moans
  from the pit —
after that woman and I anyway stop raking each other with the meat-hooks we've
  become with each other,
I fit my forehead into the smudge I've already sweated onto the window with a
  thousand other exhaustions
and watch an old man having breakfast out of a pile of bags on my front step.
Peas from a can, bread with the day-old price scrawled over the label in big letters
and then a bottle that looks so delectable, the way he carefully unsheathes it
so the neck just lips out of the wrinkled foreskin of the paper and closes his eyes
  and tilts,
long and hard, that if there were one lie left in me to forgive a last rapture
  of cowardice
I'd go down there too and sprawl and let the whole miserable rest go to pieces,
Does anyone still want to hear how love can turn rotten?
How you can be so desperate that even going adrift wouldn't be enough —
you want to scour yourself out, get rid of all the needs you've still got in yourself
that keep you endlessly tearing against yourself in rages of guilt and frustration?
I don't. I'd rather think about other things. Beauty. How do you learn to believe
  there's beauty?
The kids going by on their way to school with their fat little lunch bags: beauty!
My old drunk with his bags — bottle bags, rag bags, shoe bags: beauty! beauty!
He lies there like the goddess of wombs and first-fruit, asleep in the riches,
one hand still hooked in mid-flight over the intricacies of the iron railing.
Old father, wouldn't it be a good ending if you and I could just walk away
  together?

Or that you were the king who reveals himself, who folds back the barbed, secret wings
and we're all so in love now, one spirit, one flesh, one generation, that the truces don't matter?
Or maybe a better ending would be that there is no ending.
Maybe the Master of Endings is wandering down through his herds to find it
and the cave cow who tells truth and the death cow who holds sea in her eyes are still there
but all he hears are the same old irresistible slaughter-pen bawlings.
So maybe there is no end to the story and maybe there's no story.
Maybe the last calf just ambles up to the trough through the clearing
and nudges aside the things that swarm on the water and her mouth dips in among them and drinks.
Then she lifts, and it pours, everything, gushes, and we're lost in both waters.

The Last Deaths

1.

A few nights ago I was half-watching the news on television and half-reading to
    my daughter.
The book was about a boy who makes a zoo out of junk he finds in a lot —
I forget exactly; a horse-bottle, a bedspring that's a snake, things like that —
and on the news they were showing a film about the most recent bombings.
There was a woman crying, tearing at her hair and breasts, shrieking
    incomprehensibly
because her husband and all her children had been killed the night before
and just when she'd flung herself against the legs of one of the soldiers watching
    her,
Jessie looked up and said, "What's the matter with her? Why's she crying?"

2.

I haven't lived with my daughter for a year now and sometimes it still hurts not
    to be with her more,
not to have her laughter when I want it or to be able to comfort her when she
    cries out in her sleep.
I don't see her often enough to be able to know what I can say to her,
what I can solve for her without introducing more confusions than there were in
    the first place.
That's what happened with death. She was going to step on a bug and when I
    told her she'd kill it,
it turned out that no one had ever told her about death and now she had to know.
"It's when you don't do anything anymore," I told her. "It's like being asleep."

I didn't say for how long but she's still been obsessed with it since then,
wanting to know if she's going to die and when and if I am and her mother and
    grandma and do robbers do it?
Maybe I should have just given her the truth, but I didn't: now what was I going
    to say about that woman?
"Her house fell down," I said. "Who knocked down her house?" "It just fell."
Then I found something for us to do but last night, again, first thing,
"Tell me about that girl." "What girl?" "You know." Of course I know.
What could have gone on in my child's dreams last night so that woman was a
    girl now?
How many times must they have traded places back and forth in that innocent
    crib?
"You mean the lady whose house fell down?" "Yeah, who knocked her house
    down?"

3.

These times. The endless wars. The hatreds. The vengefulness.
Everyone I know getting out of their marriage. Old friends distrustful.
The politicians using us until you can't think about it anymore because you can't
    tell anymore
which reality affects which and how do you escape from it without everything
    battering you back again?
How many times will I lie to Jessie about things that have no meaning for either
    of us?
How many forgivenesses will I need from her when all I wanted was to keep her
    from suffering the same ridiculous illusions I have?
There'll be peace soon.
They'll fling it down like sick meat we're supposed to lick up and be thankful for
    and what then?

4.

Jessie, it's as though the whole race is sunk in an atmosphere of blood
and it's been clotting for so many centuries we can hardly move now.

Someday, you and I will face each other and turn away and the absence,
the dread, will flame between us like an enormous, palpable word that wasn't
    spoken.
Do we only love because we're weak and murderous?
Are we commended to each other to alleviate our terror of solitude and
    annihilation and that's all?

5.

I wish I could change dreams with you, baby. I've had the bad ones, what comes
    now is calm and abstract.
Last night, while you and that poor woman were trading deaths like horrible toys,
I was dreaming about the universe. The whole universe was happening in one day,
    like a blossom,
and during that day people's voices kept going out to it, crying, "Stop! Stop!"
The universe didn't mind, though. It knew we were only cursing love again
because we didn't know how to love, not even for a day,
but our little love days were just seeds it blew out on parachutes into the summer
    wind.
Then you and I were there. We shouted "Stop!" too. We kept wanting the
    universe to explode,
we kept wishing it would go back into its root, but the universe understood.
We were its children. It let us cry into its petals, it let its stems bend against us,
then it fed and covered us and we looked up sleepily — it was time to sleep —
and whatever our lives were, our love, this once, was enough.

The Race of the Flood

The way someone stays home, that's all, stays in the house, in the room, just
    stays,
the way she, let it be she this time, the way she stays, through the class, the
    backseat and the job;
the way she stays there for so many chapters, so many reels, not moving, the way
    the earth doesn't move;
the way one morning, one day, any day, she wakes and knows now that it's gone
    now,
that never is now, and she thinks she can feel it, the never, even her cells have
    spread over the sheets;
the way she thinks that oh, even these open-pored pores, even these glances
    butting the wall like thrown-away combs;
the way she, or these, these pores, glances, presences, so me, so within me,
as though I were she, exactly, as though I were the absence, too, the loss, too,
as though just beneath me was the worn, soft tallow, the unmoved and unmoving;
so there is this within me which has never touched life, never, never gone to the
    ball or the war,
never and never, so within and next and around me, fear and fear and the self-
    deceived,
the turned to the wall, the stricken, untouched, begun ill or never begun,
the way it happens without happening, begins or doesn't, moves, gives way, or
    never does.

Or this. Messages, codes; the way he, the next one, the way he pins them all over
    himself,
on his clothes, on his skin, and then walks through the street like a signpost,
    a billboard;

the way there are words to his wife and words to his kids, words even to god so
    our lord
is over his eyes and our father over his belly and the history of madness and
    history of cliffs;
the way there's no room now, the way every word in the world has stuck to the
    skin
and is used up now, and his eyes move, roll, spin up to the top of his head
the way the eyes of those fish who try to see god or the lid of the water roll,
    like dice,
so me, within me again: I cover myself with my own scrawl and wait in the
    shallow,
I face the shallow and wait like a fin and I ripple the membrane of scrawl
    like water;
so me, we, dear life I love you where are you, so we, dear our lord of anguish
    where are you,
so zero, so void; we don't even know how to end it, how to get out of the way
    of the serif or slash.

And the next, and the next, the way the next, the way all, any, any he, any
    she,
any human or less or more, if not bone that leaps with its own word then still
    more,
if not skin that washes its own wound then more and more, the way more than a
    wound,
more than a thing which has to be spoken or born, born now, later, again,
the way desire is born and born, the desire within me and not, within and with-
    out and neither;
the way the next holds onto itself and the one after holds onto me, onto my
    person, my human,
and I give back, the way ten times a day I offer it back with love or resentment
    or horror,
so I bear my likeness and greet my like, and the way will, my will or not,
the way all it can say is I am or am not, or I don't, won't, cannot or will not,
and the way that it burns anyway, and the way it smiles, smiles anyway, fills,
    ripens,

so that the hour or the scrawl burns and ripens; so within me, as though I had
   risen,
as though I had gone to the gate and opened the lock and stepped through;
so within me, it lifts and goes through, lifts itself through, and burns, anyway,
   smiles, anyway.

Bob

If you put in enough hours in bars, sooner or later you get to hear every
    imaginable kind of bullshit.
Every long-time loser has a history to convince you he isn't living at the end of his
    own leash
and every kid has some pimple on his psyche he's trying to compensate for with
    an epic,
but the person with the most unlikely line I'd ever heard — he told me he'd killed,
    more than a few times,
during the war and then afterwards working for the mob in Philadelphia — I could
    never make up my mind about.
He was big, bigger than big. He'd also been drinking hard and wanted to be
    everyone's friend
and until the bartender called the cops because he wouldn't stop stuffing money
    in girls' blouses,
he gave me his life: the farm childhood, the army, re-upping, the war — that
    killing —
coming back and the new job — that killing — then almost being killed himself by
    another hood and a kind of pension,
a distributorship, incredibly enough, for hairdresser supplies in the ward around
    Passyunk and Mifflin.
He left before the cops came and before he left he shook my hand and looked into
    my eyes.
It's impossible to tell how much that glance weighed: it was like having to lift
    something,
something so ponderous and unwieldy that you wanted to call for someone to help
    you

and when he finally turned away, it wouldn't have bothered me at all if I'd never
     seen him again.

This is going to get a little nutty now, maybe because everything was a little
     nutty for me back then.
Not a little. I'd been doing some nice refining. No work, no woman, hardly any
     friends left.
The details don't matter. I was helpless, self-pitying, angry, inert, and right now
I was flying to Detroit to interview for a job I knew I wouldn't get. Outside,
the clouds were packed against our windows and just as I let my book drop to
     look out,
we broke through into a sky so brilliant that I had to close my eyes against the glare.
I stayed like that, waiting for the stinging after-light to fade, but it seemed to pulse
     instead,
then suddenly it washed strangely through me, swelling, powdering,
and when my sight came back, I was facing inwards, into the very center of
     myself,
a dark, craggy place, and there was a sound that when I blocked the jets,
the hiss of the pressurization valves and the rattling silverware and glasses,
     I realized was laughter.
The way I was then, I think nothing could have shocked me. I was a well, I'd
     fallen in,
someone was there with me, but all I did was drift until I came to him: a figure,
     arms lifted,
he was moving in a great, cumbersome dance, full of patience, full of time, and
     that laughter,
a deep, flowing tumult of what seemed to be songs from someone else's life.
Now the strange part. My ears were ringing, my body felt like water, but I
     moved again,
farther in, until I saw the face of who it was with me and it was Bob, the drunk,
or if it wasn't him, his image filled the space, the blank, the template, better than
     anyone else
and so, however doubtful it seems now, I let it be him: he was there, I let him
     stay.

Understand, this happened quickly. By that night, home again, I was broken
    again,
torn, crushed on the empty halves of my bed, but for that time, from Pittsburgh,
    say,
until we braked down to the terminal in Detroit, I smiled at that self in myself,
his heavy dance, his laughter winding through the wrack and detritus of what
    I thought I was.

Bob, I don't know what happened to. He probably still makes the circuits of the
    clubs and corner bars
and there must be times when strangers listen and he can tell it, the truth or his
    nightmare of it.
"I killed people," the secret heart opening again, "and Jesus God, I didn't even
    know them."

Bread

A whole section of the city I live in has been urban renewed, some of it torn
    down,
some restored to what it was supposed to have been a few hundred years ago.
Once you could've walked blocks without hearing English, now the ghettos have
    been cleared,
there are parks and walkways and the houses are all owned by people who've
    moved back from the suburbs.
When I lived there, at the very edge of it where the expressway is going in now
and the buildings are still boarded with plywood or flattened altogether,
the old market was already shuttered, the shipping depots had been relocated
    upriver
and the only person I ever saw was a grocer who lived across from me over his
    empty store.
I couldn't understand what he was doing there — it must have been years
since a customer had come in past the dead register and the ice-box propped open
    with a carton,
but it was comforting to have him: he'd make his bed, sweep, cook for himself like
    a little wife
and when the constables came every week or so to tell us we were condemned,
he never paid attention so I didn't either. I didn't want to leave. I'd been in love,
I thought I was healing, for all I know I might have stayed forever in the grim
    room I was camped in
but one day some boys who must have climbed up through one of the abandoned
    tenements
suddenly appeared skidding and wrestling over the steep pitch of the old man's
    roof

and when I shouted at them to get the hell off, he must have thought I'd meant
     him:
he lurched in his bed and stopped rubbing himself with the white cream he used
     to use on his breasts.
He looked up, our eyes met, and I think for the first time he really believed I was
     there.
I don't know how long we stared at each other — I could hear the kids shrieking
     at me
and the road-building equipment that had just started tearing the skin from the
     avenue —
then his zincy fingers slowly subsided against his heart and he smiled,
a brilliant, total, incongruous smile, and even though I had no desire to,
the way afterwards I had no desire to cry when my children were born, but did,
sobbed, broke down with joy or some inadmissible apprehension, I smiled back.
It was as though we were lovers, as though, like lovers, we'd made speech again
and were listening as it gutted and fixed the space between us and then a violent,
almost physical loathing took me, for all I'd done to have ended in this place,
to myself, to everyone, to the whole business we're given the name life for.

I could go on with this. I could call it a victory, an exemplary triumph, but I'd lie.
Sometimes the universe inside us can assume the aspect of places we've been
so that instead of emotions we see trees we knew or touched or a path,
and instead of the face of a thought, there'll be an unmade bed, a car nosing from
     an alley.
All I know about that time is that it stayed, that something, pain or the fear of it,
makes me stop the wheel and reach to the silence beyond my eyes and it's still
     there:
the empty wind, the white crosses of the renewers slashed on the doorposts,
the last, dim layers of paint loosening from the rotted sills, drifting downwards.

Near the Haunted Castle

Teen Gangs Fight: Girl Paralyzed By Police Bullet — Headline

This is a story. You don't have to think about it, it's make-believe.

It's like a lie, maybe not quite a lie but I don't want you to worry about it.

The reason it's got to be a lie is because you already know the truth and I
    already know it

and what difference does it make? We still can't do anything: why kill yourself?

So here's the story. It's like the princess and the pea, remember?

Where they test her with mattresses and a pea and she's supposed not to sleep

and get upset and then they'll know she's the princess and marry her?

Except in this version, she comes in and nobody believes it's her and they lay her
    down

but instead of forty mattresses do you know what they lay her on? Money!

Of course, money! A million dollars! It's like a hundred mattresses, it's so soft,
    a thousand!

It's how much you cut from the budget for teachers to give the policemen.

It's how much you take from relief to trade for bullets. Soft!

And instead of the pea, what? A bullet! Brilliant! A tiny bullet stuck in at the
    bottom!

So then comes the prince. My prince, my beauty. Except he has holsters.

He has leather and badges. And what he does, he starts tearing the mattresses
    out.

Out? Don't forget, it's a story. Don't forget to not worry, it's pretend.

He's tearing the mattresses out and then he's stuffing them in his mouth!

This wonderful prince-mouth, this story-mouth, it holds millions, billions,

and she's falling, slowly, or no, the pea, the bullet, is rising,

surging like some ridiculous funny snout out of the dark down there.

Does it touch you? Oh, yes, but don't worry, this is just a fib, right?

It slides next to your skin and it's cold and it goes in, in! as though you were
     a door,
as though you were the whole bedroom; in, through the backbone, through the
     cartilage,
the cords, then it freezes. It freezes and the prince is all gone,
this is the sleeping, the wrong-sleeping, you shouldn't be sleeping,
the so-heaviness in the arms, the so-heaviness in the legs, don't sleep, they'll leave
     you,
they'll throw you away . . . the dollars spinning, the prince leaving,
and you, at the bottom, on the no-turning, on the pea, like a story,
on the bullet, the single bullet that costs next to nothing, like one dollar.
People torture each other so they'll tell the whole truth, right?
And study the nervous systems of the lower orders to find the truth, right?
And tell the most obviously absurd tales for the one grain of truth?
The mother puts down her book and falls asleep watching television.
On the television they go on talking.
The father's in bed, the little gears still rip through his muscles.
The two brothers have the same dream, like Blinken and Nod, like the mayor and
     the president.
The sister . . . The sister . . . The heart furnace, the brain furnace, hot . . .
     hot . . .
Let's go back to find where the truth is. Let's find the beginning.
In the beginning was love, right? No, in the beginning . . . the bullet . . .

The Cave

I think most people are relieved the first time they actually know someone who
   goes crazy.
It doesn't happen the way you hear about it where the person gibbers and sticks
   to you like an insect:
mostly there's crying, a lot of silence, sometimes someone will whisper back to
   their voices.
All my friend did was sit, at home until they found him, then for hours at a time
   on his bed in the ward,
pointing at his eyes, chanting the same phrase over and over. "Too much fire!"
   he'd say. "Too much fire!"
I remember I was amazed at how raggedy he looked, then annoyed because he
   wouldn't answer me
and then, when he was getting better, I used to pester him to tell me about that
   fire-thing.
He'd seemed to be saying he'd seen too much and I wanted to know too much
   what
because my obsession then was that I was somehow missing everything beyond the
   ordinary.
What was only real was wrong. There were secrets that could turn you into stone,
they were out of range or being kept from me, but my friend, if he knew what I
   meant, wouldn't say,
so we'd talk politics or books or moon over a beautiful girl who was usually in the
   visiting room when we were
who mutilated herself. Every time I was there, new slashes would've opened out
   over her forearms and wrists
and once there were two brilliant medallions on her cheeks that I thought were
   rouge spots

but that my friend told me were scratches she'd put there with a broken light bulb
 when she'd run away the day before.
The way you say running away in hospitals is "eloping." Someone who hurts
 themself is a "cutter."
How could she do it to herself? My friend didn't think that was the question.
She'd eloped, cut, they'd brought her back and now she was waiting there again,
those clowny stigmata of lord knows what on her, as tranquil and seductive as ever.
I used to storm when I'd leave her there with him. She looked so vulnerable.
All the hours they'd have. I tormented myself imagining how they'd come
 together,
how they'd tell each other the truths I thought I had to understand to live,
then how they'd kiss, their lips, chaste and reverent, rushing over the forgiven
 surfaces.
Tonight, how long afterwards, watching my wife undress, letting my gaze go so
 everything blurs
but the smudges of her nipples and hair and the wonderful lumpy graces of her
 pregnancy,
I still can bring it back: those dismal corridors, the furtive nods, the moans I
 thought were sexual
and the awful lapses that seemed vestiges of exaltations I would never have,
but now I know whatever in the mystery I was looking for, whatever brute or cloud
 I thought eluded me,
isn't lost in the frenzy of one soul or another, but next to us, in the touch,
 between.
Lying down, fumbling for the light, moving into the shadow with my son or
 daughter, I find it again:
the prism of hidden sorrow, the namelessness of nothing and nothing shuddering
 across me,
and then the warmth, clinging and brightening, the hide, the caul, the first mind.

Hog Heaven

FOR JAMES HAVARD

It stinks. It stinks and it stinks and it stinks and it stinks.
It stinks in the mansions and it stinks in the shacks and the carpeted offices,
in the beds and the classrooms and out in the fields where there's no one.
It just stinks. Sniff and feel it come up: it's like death coming up.
Take one foot, ignore it long enough, leave it on the ground long enough
because you're afraid to stop, even to love, even to be loved,
it'll stink worse than you can imagine, as though the whole air was meat pressing
    your eyelids,
as though you'd been caught, hung up from the earth
and all the stinks of the fear drain down and your toes are the valves dripping
the giant stinks of the pain and the death and the radiance.
Old people stink, with their teeth and their hot rooms, and the kiss,
the age-kiss, the death-kiss, it comes like a wave and you want to fall down and be
    over.
And money stinks: the little threads that go through it like veins through an eye,
each stinks — if you hold it onto your lip it goes bad, it stinks like a vein going
    bad.
And Christ stank: he knew how the slaves would be stacked into the holds and he
    took it —
the stink of the vomit and shit and of somebody just rolling over and plunging in
    with his miserable seed.
And the seed stinks. And the fish carrying it upstream and the bird eating the
    fish
and you the bird's egg, the dribbles of yolk, the cycle: the whole thing stinks.
The intellect stinks and the moral faculty, like things burning, like the cave under
    justice,

and the good quiet men, like oceans of tears squeezed into one handful, they stink,
and the whole consciousness, like something plugged up, stinks, like something
    cut off.
Life stinks and death stinks and god and your hand touching your face
and every breath, daring to turn, daring to come back from the stop: the turn
    stinks
and the last breath, the real one, the one where everyone troops into your bed
and piles on — oh, that one stinks best! It stays on your mouth
and who you kiss now knows life and knows death, knows how it would be to
    fume in a nostril
and the thousand desires that stink like the stars and the voice heard through
    the stars
and each time — milk sour, egg sour, sperm sour — each time — dirt, friend,
    father —
each time — mother, tree, breath — each time — breath and breath and breath —
each time the same stink, the amazement, the wonder to do this and it flares,
this, and it stinks, this: it stinks and it stinks and it stinks and it stinks.

The Shade

A summer cold. No fever. Nothing. But a dozen times during the night I wake
to listen to my son whimpering in his sleep, trying to snort the sticky phlegm out
    of his nostrils.
The passage clears, silence, nothing. I cross the room, groping for the warm,
elusive creature of his breath and my heart lunges, stutters, tries to race away;
I don't know from what, from my imagination, from life itself, maybe from
    understanding too well
and being unable to do anything about how much of my anxiety is always for
    myself.
Whatever it was, I left it when the dawn came. There's a park near here
where everyone who's out of work in our neighborhood comes to line up in the
    morning.
The converted schoolbuses shuttling hands to the cannery fields in Jersey were
    just rattling away when I got there
and the small-time contractors, hiring out cheap walls, cheap ditches, cheap
    everything,
were loading laborers onto the sacks of plaster and concrete in the backs of their
    pickups.
A few housewives drove by looking for someone to babysit or clean cellars for
    them,
then the gates of the local bar unlaced and whoever was left drifted in out of the
    wall of heat
already rolling in with the first fists of smoke from the city incinerators.

It's so quiet now, I can hear the sparrows foraging scraps of garbage on the paths.
The stove husk chained as a sign to the store across the street creaks in the last
    breeze of darkness.

By noon, you'd have to be out of your mind to want to be here: the park will reek of urine,

bodies will be sprawled on the benches, men will wrestle through the surf of broken bottles,

but even now, watching the leaves of the elms softly lifting toward the day, softly falling back,

all I see is fear forgiving fear on every page I turn; all I know is every time I try to change it,

I say it again: my wife, my child . . . my home, my work, my sorrow.

If this were the last morning of the world, if time had finally moved inside us and erupted

and we were Agamemnon again, Helen again, back on that faint, beginning planet

where even the daily survivals were giants, filled with light, I think I'd still be here,

afraid or not enough afraid, silently howling the names of death over the grass and asphalt.

The morning goes on, the sun burning, the earth burning, and between them, part of me lifts and starts back,

past the wash of dead music from the bar, the drinker reeling on the curb, the cars coughing alive,

and part, buried in itself, stays, forever, blinking into the glare, freezing.

With Ignorance

With ignorance begins a knowledge the first characteristic of which is ignorance.

KIERKEGAARD

1.

Again and again. Again lips, again breast, again hand, thigh, loin and bed and
    bed
after bed, the hunger, hunger again, need again, the rising, the spasm and needing
    again.
Flesh, lie, confusion and loathing, the scabs of clear gore, the spent seed and the
    spurt
of desire that seemed to generate from itself, from its own rising and spasm.
Everything waste, everything would be or was, the touching, the touch and the
    touch back.
Everything rind, scar, without sap, without meaning or seed, and everyone,
    everyone else,
every slip or leap into rage, every war, flame, sob, it was there, too, the stifling,
    the hushed,
malevolent frenzy and croak of desire, again and again, the same hunger, same
    need.
Touch me, hold me, sorrow and sorrow, the emptied, emptied again, touched again.
The hunger, the rising, again and again until again itself seemed to be need and
    hunger
and so much terror could rise out of that, the hunger repeating itself out of the
    fear now,
that how could you know if you lived within it at all, if there wasn't another,
a malediction or old prayer, a dream or a city of dream or a single, fleshless,
    dreamless error,

whose tongue you were, who spoke with you, butted or rasped with you, but still, tongue or another,

word or not word, what could it promise that wouldn't drive us back to the same hunger and sorrow?

What could it say that wouldn't spasm us back to ourselves to be bait or a dead prayer?

Or was that it? Only that? The prayer hunting its prey, hunting the bait of itself?

Was the hunger the faith in itself, the belief in itself, even the prayer?

Was it the dead prayer?

2.

The faces waver; each gathers the others within it, the others shuddering through it

as though there were tides or depths, as though the depths, the tides of the eyes themselves

could throw out refractions, waves, shifts and wavers and each faceless refraction

could rise to waver beneath me, to shift, to be faceless again, beneath or within me,

the lying, confusion, recurrence, reluctance, the surge through into again.

Each room, each breast finding its ripeness of shadow, each lip and its shadow,

the dimming, flowing, the waver through time, through loss, gone, irredeemable,

all of it, each face into regret, each room into forgetting and absence.

But still, if there were a moment, still, one moment, to begin in or go back to,

to return to move through, waver through, only a single moment carved back from the lie

the way the breast is carved from its shadow, sealed from the dross of darkness

until it takes the darkness itself and fills with it, taking the breath;

if, in the return, I could be taken the way I could have been taken, with voice or breast,

emptied against the space of the breast as though breast was breath and my breath,

taken, would have been emptied into the moment, it could rise here, now, in that moment, the same moment.

But it won't, doesn't. The moments lift and fall, break, and it shifts, wavers, subsides into the need again, the faceless again, the faceless and the lie.

3.

Remorse? Blame? There is a pit-creature. The father follows it down with the ax.
Exile and sorrow. Once there were things we lived in, don't you remember?
We scraped, starved, then we came up, abashed, to the sun, and what was the first
    word?
Blame, blame and remorse, then sorrow, then the blame was the father then was
    ourselves.
Such a trite story, do we have to retell it? The mother took back the sun and
    we . . .
Remorse, self-regard, call it shame or being abashed or trying again, for the last
    time, to return.
Remorse, then power, the power and the blame and what did we ever suffer but
    power?
The head lifting itself, then the wars, remorse and revenge, the wars of humility,
the blades and the still valley, the double intention, the simple tree in the blood.
Then exile again, even the sword, even the spear, the formula scratched on the
    sand,
even the christening, the christened, blame again, power again, but even then,
taken out of the fire at the core and never returned, what could we not sanction?
One leg after the other, the look back, the power, the fire again and the sword
    again.
Blame and remorse. That gives into desire again, into hunger again. That gives
    into . . . this . . .

4.

Someone . . . Your arm touches hers or hers finds yours, unmoving, unasking.
A silence, as though for the first time, and, as though for the first time, you can
    listen,

as though there were chords: your life, then the other's, someone else, as though
for the first time.
The life of the leaves over the streetlamp and the glow, swelling, chording, under
the shadows,
and the quaver of things built, one quavering cell at a time, and the song
of the cell gently bedding itself in its mortar, in this silence, this first attempting.
Even the shush of cars, the complex stress of a step, the word called into the
darkness,
and, wait, the things even beyond, beyond membrane or awareness, mode, sense,
dream,
don't they sing, too? Chord, too? Isn't the song and the silence there, too?
I heard it once. It changed nothing, but once, before I went on, I did hear:
the equation of star and plant, the wheel, the ecstasy and division, the equation
again.
The absolute walking its planks, its long wall, its long chord of laughter or grief.
I heard silence, then the children, the spawn, how we have to teach every cell
how to speak,
and from that, after that, the kiss back from the speech, the touch back from the
song.
And then more, I heard how it alters, how we, the speakers, the can't-live, the
refuse-to,
how we, only in darkness, groaning and thrashing into the undergrowth of our
eternal,
would speak then, would howl, howl again, and at last, at the end, we'd hear it:
the prayer and the flesh crying *Why aren't you here?* And the cry back in it,
I am! I am!

5.

Imagine dread. Imagine, without symbol, without figure, history or histories;
a place, not a place.
Imagine it must be risen through, beginning with the silent moment, the secrets
quieted,
one hour, one age at a time, sadness, nostalgia, the absurd pain of betrayal.

34

Through genuine grief, then, through the genuine suffering for the boundaries
    of self
and the touch on the edge, the compassion, that never, never quite, breaks
    through.
Imagine the touch again and beyond it, beyond either end, joy or terror, either
    ending,
the context that gives way, not to death, but past, past anything still with a name,
even death, because even death is a promise offering comfort, solace, that any
    direction we turn,
there'll still be the word, the name, and this the promise now, even with terror,
the promise again that the wordlessness and the self won't be for one instant the
    same enacting,
and we stay within it, a refusal now, a turning away, a never giving way,
we stay until even extinction itself, the absence, death itself, even death, isn't
    longed for,
never that, but turned toward in the deepest turn of the self, the deepest gesture
    toward self.
And then back, from the dread, from locution and turn, from whatever history
    reflects us,
the self grounds itself again in itself and reflects itself, even its loss, as its own,
and back again, still holding itself back, the certainty and belief tearing again,
back from the edge of that one flood of surrender which, given space, would, like
    space itself,
rage beyond any limit, the flesh itself giving way in its terror, and back from
    that,
into love, what we have to call love, the one moment before we move onwards
    again,
toward the end, the life again of the self-willed, self-created, embodied, reflected
    again.
Imagine a space prepared for with hunger, with dread, with power and the power
over dread which is dread, and the love, with no space for itself, no power for
    itself,
a moment, a silence, a rising, the terror for that, the space for that. Imagine love.

6.

Morning. The first morning of now. You, your touch, your song and morning,
    but still,
something, a last fear or last lie or last clench of confusion clings,
holds back, refuses, resists, the way fear itself clings in its web of need or dread.
What would release be? Being forgiven? No, never forgiven, never only forgiven.
To be touched, somehow, with presence, so that the only sign is a step, towards
    or away?
Or not even a step, because the walls, of self, of dread, can never release,
can never forgive stepping away, out of the willed or refused, out of the lie or the
    fear
of the self that still holds back and refuses, resists, and turns back again and again
    into the willed.
What if it could be, though? The first, hectic rush past guilt or remorse?
What if we could find a way through the fires that aren't with us and the terrors
    that are?
What would be there? Would we be thrown back into perhaps or not yet or not
    needed or done?
Could we even slip back, again, past the first step into the first refusal,
the first need, first blot of desire that still somehow exists and wants to resist,
    wants to give back the hard,
immaculate shell of the terror it still keeps against respite and unclenching?
Or perhaps no release, no step or sign, perhaps only to wait and accept.
Perhaps only to bless. To bless and to bless and to bless and to bless.
Willed or unwilled, word or sign, the word suddenly filled with its own breath.
Self and other the self within other and the self still moved through its word,
consuming itself, still, and consuming, still being rage, war, the fear, the aghast,
but bless, bless still, even the fear, the loss, the gutting of word, the gutting even
    of hunger,
but still to bless and bless, even the turn back, the refusal, to bless and to bless and
    to bless.

7.

The first language was loss, the second sorrow, this is the last, then: yours . . .
An island, summer, late dusk; hills, laurel and thorn. I walked from the harbor,
    over the cliff road,
down the long trail through the rocks. When I came to our house the ship's wake
    was just edging onto the shore
and on the stone beach, under the Cypress, the low waves reassuming themselves
    in the darkness, I waited.
There was a light in a room. You came to it, leaned to it, reaching, touching,
and watching you, I saw you give back to the light a light more than light
and to the silence you gave more than silence, and, in the silence, I heard it.
You, your self, your life, your beginning, pleasure, song clear as the light that
    touched you.
Your will, your given and taken; grief, recklessness, need, or desire.
Your passion or tear, step forward or step back into the inevitable veil.
Yours and yours and yours, the dream, the wall of the self that won't be or
    needn't be breached,
and the breach, the touch, yours and the otherness, yours, the separateness,
never giving way, never breached really, but as simple, always, as light, as silence.
This is the language of that, that light and that silence, the silence rising through
    or from you.
Nothing to bless or not bless now, nothing to thank or forgive, not to triumph,
surrender, mean, reveal, assume or exhaust. Our faces bent to the light, and still,
there is terror, still history, power, grief and remorse, always, always the self and
    the other
and the endless tide, the waver, the terror again, between and beneath, but you,
    now,
your touch, your light, the otherness yours, the reach, the wheel, the waves
    touching.
And to, not wait, not overcome, not even forget or forgive the dream of the
    moment, the unattainable moment again.
Your light . . . Your silence . . .
In the silence, without listening, I heard it, and without words, without language
    or breath, I answered.